## READ WHAT PEOPLE ARE SAYING ABOUT
### *Transformed by Tough Times*

"In the aftermath of being stranded for five days following Hurricane Katrina, this book helped me so m[...] 50 copies to friends and colleagues tr[...] and broken dreams...."

[...]ass
[...]AIN
Interim LSU Public Hospital, New Orleans, Louisiana

"As a person new to faith in Jesus, I was trying to lead a Christ-led life. But worry and doubt held me back every step of the way. I was, well, STUCK! When I read Steve's book, it opened my eyes so that God could change my heart. I finally could let go of all my worry and control that I thought I had. And WOW! God made miracles begin to happen in my life. I have since given this book to friends in my small group and to several others, and they have had such a change in their hearts too. If you are going through tough times, pick up this book. It will help."

**Amanda McCanles-Crable**
HEALTH SERVICES WORKER
Belton, Missouri

"In light of today's economic uncertainties and the tough times many are facing, I heartily recommend Steve's book to Christians and Christian leaders everywhere."

**Paul Powell**
DEAN EMERITUS
George W. Truett Theological Seminary

"Nothing would please me more than to see this book become a best seller. It offers so much help to people who are hurting that it must get into the hands of as many people as possible."

**Steve Harrison**
PRESIDENT
Bradley Communications and Founder of the Million Dollar Author Club

i

"During one of Steve's down times in ministry, I invited him over to hang around our team during one of our annual leadership summits. It was a joy for us to be able to do that then. But now, it's an even greater joy to see how God has raised up Steve to help many others. This book offers help and hope to those who are hurting, and it's offered by someone who has been there."

**Adam Hamilton**
SENIOR PASTOR
United Methodist Church of the Resurrection, Leawood, Kansas.


"If you have life all together, buy this book by Steve Reed, and put the book away until you do not have life all together. A superb book for any person facing the realities of life and looking for encouragement and practical help. When the going gets tough, the truths in this book will help. Read, understand, practice, and grow to be a stronger leader. READ ON, LEAD ON."

**Charlie Baker**
INTERNAL COACH
Ernst & Young, Tulsa, Oklahoma


"Soon after Hurricane Katrina devastated New Orleans—leaving hundreds of thousands homeless and destroying entire neighborhoods, thousands of businesses, and many churches—our pastors received a shipment of Steve Reed's book on overcoming tough times. It could not have been more timely, with its outstanding insights and comforting words of healing and strength. Recently, a leader from one of our denomination's mission boards was in our city—this is over 3 years after the hurricane—and he remarked at the excellent attitude and good mental health of our pastors. He said, "I was expecting to hear a lot of 'Woe is me' and 'Why me, Lord?' but got none of that." I assured him it was because the Lord had provided a number of angels of healing and comfort who kept our people on an even keel. We're grateful for the strong role Steve's book played in that healing."

**Joe McKeever**
RETIRED DIRECTOR OF MISSIONS
The Baptist Association of Greater New Orleans

"As a horse trainer and minister to couples who are getting married, I see how the way we deal with adversity can make or break a horse, a marriage, or a life. Steve's book hit me right where I'm at—especially after I lost my wife to cancer. I heartily recommend this book to anyone who's hit a rough spell in life or who is wise enough to prepare for the next storm that's looming on the horizon."

**Gary Snider**
HORSE BROKER AND COWBOY MINISTER
Divide, Colorado

"I met Steve several years ago at a missionary training event I was leading and was drawn to his passion for church planting movements and to his deep desire to help people deal effectively with suffering. The concepts he mentions in his book are both life changing and grounded in scripture. As a mission strategist, I see people all over the world getting in touch with their "suffering clause" and doing amazing things under extraordinary conditions. Now it's time for North Americans to get it. I believe Steve can help. Read this and grow."

**Curtis Sergeant**
VICE PRESIDENT, GLOBAL STRATEGIES
e3 Partners Ministry, Plano, Texas

"Steve does a masterful job at showing us how to embrace what we tend to avoid in order to experience what we deeply desire. His asking of relevant questions coaches us to pursue our calling and at the same time flourish in our souls."

**Rick Olson**
PERSONAL AND LEADERSHIP COACH
www.coachtogrow.com

"Steve is living life to the max, and his insights for outlasting tough times are something I can identify with as a pastor."

**Vernon Armitage**
FORMER SENIOR PASTOR
Pleasant Valley Baptist Church, Liberty, Missouri
Author of *Living Life to the Max*

"As missionary colleagues of Steve's parents in Peru, we know firsthand some of the stories Steve shares, and we strongly agree with the transformational message he delivers so powerfully in this book."

**Betty and Charles Alexander**
RETIRED SBC MISSIONARIES TO CHILE AND PERU
Fort Worth, Texas

"I've known Steve for more than a decade and can affirm that what he talks about in this book, he has lived. Though you could say that suffering has marked Steve's life and ministry, it has never diminished his spirit or his willingness to pick himself up and joyfully move into the future. When Steve gave me an early copy of the book, I used it as a springboard to a series of messages at our church that were extremely well-received and helpful to many in our congregation. Pastors, you need to teach this to your leaders and folks in your congregation."

**Rick McGinniss**
SENIOR PASTOR
North Heartland Community Church, Kansas City, Missouri

"Steve exceeds all expectations with this book as he coaches us to embrace the transforming power of pain, God's gift to us."

**Linda Olson**
FOUNDER, PROFESSIONAL SPEAKER
Made for Something More
Author of *Exceeding Your Expectations*

"In 2010, God directed me to join forces with Steve in the unfolding ministry to the cowboys of Guatemala and Honduras. During the many days spent together in ministry, we have found a common bond in learning the lessons of the cross. In this book, Steve has opened his life and his heart to share a message that is vital for every believer in Jesus Christ to follow."

**Keith Moody**
COWBOY, SHEEP SHEARER
Pastor of Calvary Chapel of Colome, South Dakota

"I have walked with pastors and church leaders for over 40 years and have noticed that those who learned how to positively handle life's disappointments have been the most fruitful in their ministry. In our state convention, there are many unsung heroes who have faithfully followed God's call in some obscure and difficult places. I count Steve as one of those unsung heroes whose voice needs to be heard. His book will be helpful for anyone who faces a tough ministry challenge."

**R. Rex Lindsay**
FORMER EXECUTIVE DIRECTOR
Kansas/Nebraska Convention of Southern Baptists

"When Steve approached me about his book idea, I invited him into our circle of the Heart of America Christian Writers' Network. In the past couple of years, I've seen Steve rise rapidly in his skill as a writer. More than that, I believe he has an important message to bring to the Christian community. This book is one I'm telling people about."

**Mark Littleton**
CO-DIRECTOR
Heart of America Christian Writers' Network
Author of over 100 books, including *Never Give Up: Seven Principles for Leading in Tough Times*

"I met Steve while I was working in the marketplace and feeling called to start a church. Later, Steve invited me on his staff, and I got to see first-hand how he handled many difficult situations. Now that we've started a new church, I realize even more the role that suffering plays in the life of a leader, and I go to Steve often for advice and encouragement. I wish every pastor had a friend and a coach like Steve. Whether you are a pastor, church leader, or business leader, you need to read this book."

**Chris Pinion**
LEAD PASTOR
LifeQuest Church, Kansas City, Missouri
Co-Author of *Scars: Life Hurts God Heals*

"If you are looking to find God's vision for your life while going through a tough time, read this book. Steve is fully engaged in ministry and mission endeavors that place him at the cutting edge of effective ministry to a wide range of cultures and people groups."

**William Tinsley**
Author of *Finding God's Mission: Missions and the New Realities*

"I've enjoyed working with Steve in ministry in Guatemala and have spent countless hours discussing the topics in this book with him. His heart resonates so strongly with mine that I get excited every time we get to work together and share insights with one another. This book conveys much of what I want my walk with God to be like when I face tough times."

**Ray Gurney**
PASTOR
Cross Creek Baptist Mission, Grain Valley, Missouri

"In walking through many difficult situations with people in our church, I have noticed that the bigger and uglier the scar, the bigger the opportunity for God to do something amazing. Because Steve has worked in several capacities in our church, I have seen first hand how he's been a healing agent. But this material is more than just a tool to soothe a painful situation. With this printing our church will begin to use this book and the companion small group Bible study guides to get people together for healing and growing. If you are like us and need help with caring for your congregation, I'd recommend you take a good look at this book and the study guide that is available online."

**Karen Blankenship**
EXECUTIVE PASTOR
LifeQuest Church, Kansas City, Missouri
Co-author of *Scars: Life Hurts God Heals*

"Steve knows about tough times, and he has weathered his with grace. As a pastor who helps hurting people, I'm looking for resources like this one that is both informational and inspirational. Read it; you'll be better prepared for the thunder rumbling in the distance."

**Rod Casey**
SENIOR ASSOCIATE PASTOR
Woodcrest Chapel, Columbia, Missouri

# A NOTE FROM A FELLOW STRUGGLER

If you are reading this and are as broken as I was the first time I read this book, you may be feeling a resistance welling up in you, saying, "Steve doesn't understand. My tough times are different. God has abandoned me. I'm in a hopeless situation." I felt that way, and those feelings so choked my spirit that I almost didn't read this incredible book. For those of us who are at the bottom of difficult circumstances, we don't often trust people very well. So allow me a minute to tell you why I think Steve can be trusted to help us be transformed by our tough times.

I have known Steve since 1994, but I didn't really know him, and he didn't really know me, until June of 2008, when I was at an all-time low in my life. We had done ministry together for a couple of years in the mid 90's and had stayed in touch some after that. But when my reality crashed, Steve was one of the few who showed up to be with me.

Now, granted, Steve would like to be seen as the cowboy hero who rides into town on a powerful white stallion, with his six shooters a-blazin' to save the day. But I see him more like a faith healer. No, not the kind you might see on TV. His faith and his beliefs about people are healing in a different way. He relentlessly trusts that God has created each human being for a unique purpose. No matter what level of suffering, no matter how isolated, stuck, or wounded a person is, Steve will invest time, energy, and resources to invite responsiveness that leads to God's deep healing. Some might say he's wasting time. But Steve seems willing to encourage over and over again until God works.

At first, Steve tried to teach, exhort, and cheer me out of my anger and bitterness. In my case, that didn't work very well. But he didn't give up on me. As I reflect on what Steve did for me, I think there are some powerful things he did that really helped. First, Steve "let me be." He accepted me, and that acceptance told me that he loved me. Even when I was angry and bitter, ugly, and full of self-pity, Steve saw me through it. Somehow he seemed to delight in me—seeing me as a masterpiece in progress. In a nutshell, Steve was patient. Steve talks about the body of Christ becoming Jesus with skin on. Well, Steve was Jesus in the flesh to me during those times.

Steve did a second thing for me that was incredibly profound. He became vulnerable and invited *me* to help *him*. Though I was consumed by shame, dishonor, and a belief that I had forfeited and given up everything, Steve gave me a chance to get outside of myself and help him. Looking back, Steve trusted me even as I was untrustworthy. While he carried a lot of my burden, he gave me the dignity of helping carry his burden, too. I'm not even sure he was aware of doing that. While I doubted God and didn't trust Him, God gave Steve the courage to rely on me and let me carry him! Now that's a crucial issue–allowing someone to carry you.

A third thing I noticed about Steve was his unshakable trust in God and his belief that God had his back. I've discovered that when people believe that God has their back, they can trust other people in remarkable ways. Maybe that was why Steve could have the courage to risk relying on a wounded, hurting human being like me. Jesus demonstrated this kind of vulnerability in His ministry. He associated and ministered with some of the most unlikely people. He didn't flaunt His power and authority. He didn't start His ministry with a million dollars in the bank and people who had it all together. Jesus was vulnerable. I believe that since Jesus believed God had His back, He could allow the most broken of people to help Him. I have seen that kind of Jesus trust in Steve.

As you read this book, I invite you to invest your time, your self, and your heart–to be vulnerable and allow the Spirit of God to transform you. If you are warring in your heart like I was, I urge you to drop your defenses, lay down your weapons, and invite God to transform you through the pages of this book. When I had my defenses up, love couldn't get through to me. To overcome my resistance, Steve risked being knocked down, bloodied, and beaten for me to understand that God loves the brokenhearted. Hmm, that too sounds like a Jesus move to me.

Because of my experience with Steve, I believe that he is just beginning to tap into the gifting that God has given him in the area of healing – the healing of souls, the healing of spirits, the healing of the wounded. If you are wounded, or know someone who is, I invite you to experience the truths Steve offers. As you get started, I encourage you to follow Steve's advice to get a partner to go through this together. Take it from someone who was isolated from people for a long time. Don't go it alone. Find your Steve. Find your friend to walk with you through your tough times. If you can't find somebody you know, then I'd suggest you try a homeless shelter, a nursing home, a hospital, or some other likely place to find someone who's also wounded, and walk through the tough times together with them.

For your own sake, and for the sake of others you might impact down the road, hang on, my friend. Keep reading. Hope could be just a few pages away.

**Bill Burrows**
Steve's friend and fellow struggler

# TRANSFORMED BY TOUGH TIMES

STEVE REED

# TRANSFORMED BY TOUGH TIMES

© 2012 by Steve Reed

Originally printed in 2005 under the title:
*The Suffering Clause: a Leader's Surprising Secret for Outlasting Tough Times*

Published by Reed Group Publishing
11628 Oakmont, Suite 102
Overland Park, KS 66210

Printed in the United States of America

Cover design by Reed Website Design
Josh Reed, Designer

Reed, Steve, 2012

Transformed by Tough Times

ISBN 978-0-9773251-3-9

To order additional copies go to
**www.TransformedbyToughTimes.com**.

# SPECIAL MESSAGE TO READERS...

When I wrote the first edition of this book, I felt that my primary audience was Christian leaders. At the time, I was in the middle of pastoring a church, and I loved going to leadership conferences. So the original title of this book was *The Suffering Clause: a Leader's Surprising Secret for Outlasting Tough Times.* But a funny thing happened after we printed and began to distribute the book. Readers who weren't involved in formal ministry got copies and began to give me feedback. Actually, "feedback" is too nice of a word. They scolded me! Some told me in person, and some emailed me to say that my book applied to a much wider audience than my title let on.

So to my friends who chastised me, your wish is now granted! *Transformed by Tough Times* is my humble attempt to offer a work that can help just about anyone who is faced with some tough circumstances. I've added a couple of completely new chapters to the previous edition and have sprinkled in new material throughout. Please be aware that, in spite of my best efforts to widen the net here, a lot of the original material aimed at pastors and church leaders is still there. Because I believe that every Christian is a minister and that there shouldn't even be a distinction between laity and clergy in the church, I don't regret leaving a lot of the leadership implications included just like it was in the original. If you read this version and feel that I could improve it for future editions, keep those cards and letters coming! I welcome feedback.

In addition to widening the audience, I've also attempted to make this material more user friendly for small groups to experience together. Note that we offer free downloads of the *Transformed by Tough Times* small group material. You can find it on the website at www.TransformedbyToughTimes.com.

Also, on the following page, you'll notice a pact for you to sign with a partner. I've seen firsthand how those who go through a book like this one with a friend will greatly enhance their absorption of the material and will increase their likelihood of experiencing positive and lasting changes. If you know someone who might be interested in going through this with you, invite them to sign with you on your pact. If they have their own book, offer to reciprocate signing with them.

As you begin to read, I hope you see how you really can be transformed, not just *in spite of* your tough times, but actually *because of* your tough times. Could it be that right now, in the middle of your darkest night, God is holding out a candle of hope for you?

Get ready to be transformed.

**Steve**

# MY PACT

I commit to the process of discovering how I can be transformed, not just *in spite of* my tough times, but *because of* my tough times. As I seek help and support for myself, I also commit to being supportive and helpful to others who are challenged with difficult circumstances as well.

_____

**Your name**

_____

**Partner's name**

**Steve Reed**

_____

*"It's better to have a partner than go it alone.*
*Share the work, share the wealth.*
*And if one falls down, the other helps,*
*But if there's no one to help, tough!*

*By yourself you're unprotected.*
*With a friend you can face the worst.*
*Can you round up a third?*
*A three-stranded rope isn't easily snapped."*

**King Solomon**
Ecclesiastes 4:9-12 (The Message)

# DEDICATED TO...

I wholeheartedly dedicate this book to my wife Nola, who, for more than 27 years, has joyfully and sacrificially walked with me through many difficult life and ministry situations. I am amazed and grateful that she has done it with a genuine smile on her face and a song in her heart. Thanks, Nola!

For more cartoons by Joe McKeever, go to **www.JoeMcKeever.com**.

# TABLE OF CONTENTS

## BOOK I: THE SUFFERING CLAUSE

## BOOK II: TRANSFORMED BY TOUGH TIMES

# FOREWORD

Even though it may not look like it, the book that you hold in your hands is really two books. Believe me, I didn't mean to write two books! If I had known that's what I was doing when I started writing, I would have probably asked you to shoot me and put me out of my misery! But as I wrote, I realized that there were actually two big ideas that I couldn't let go of if I were to give you the best I had to offer. And the more I wrote, the more convinced I became that the two needed to become one. Each big idea completes the other.

The first book consists of material that introduces the concept of "the suffering clause." To do that, I weave in some of my story while I build a biblical case for this idea. Along the way, we lean heavily on the Apostle Paul and Jesus, and see how much of their teachings on suffering have played out in the lives of many heroic people—both in the Bible, and in our own day.

In the second book I offer hope to those who are hurting. In this section, we take a closer look at the individual who suffers and deal more in depth with the problem of pain and suffering. This book offers us a handle on some of the more difficult situations we face where suffering just doesn't make sense.

I have one word of advice as you begin to read. It might be tempting to gloss over the quotes and scriptures that precede each chapter in order to get to the "meat." I beg you not to do that. Linger a bit over those words. Some of the quotes might make you chuckle, others may offer a hook to hold onto a truth that you are about to receive. Often the real "meat" is in that material—especially in the scriptures. I have merely tried to cut off a few pieces of it for you to sample. Chew on some of those passages for yourself. Look up some of the scriptures that strike you, and savor the greater context of the stories where those texts reside. Ask the Holy Spirit to feed you beyond what I have cooked up for you on these pages. See if there aren't some delicious meals that the Lord might give you that come directly from Him. Then be sure to share your thoughts with someone else. Whether you read this alone or with others, a good discussion over the material will only add to your insight and will help you the most when you need someone to walk alongside you for encouragement in the transformations God is prompting you to make.

I pray that this book feeds your soul—helping you see suffering in a whole new light. May it provide you with nourishment to strengthen your faith, increase your endurance, build lifelong friends, and help you feel God's pleasure as you seek to finish strong in what God has called you to do.

# BOOK I

# THE SUFFERING CLAUSE

*"For me, to live is Christ and to die is gain."*
**— The Apostle Paul, Philippians 1:21**

PART ONE

# My Story
# and the
# Suffering Clause

# Chapter One: Think About What You're Thinking About...

*As a man thinks in his heart, so is he...*
Proverbs 23:7 (adapted from the KJV)

Suffering. Unlike Visa, it's everywhere you *don't* want to be.

The game is on the line. We are behind. Seconds are left on the clock. The coach looks at me and hollers, "Field goal!" I trot onto the field and line up for the kick. If I make it, we win. If I miss, we lose. The next day in the paper my name will be associated with "fame" or "blame."

As I stand in anticipation—quaking in my cleats—I pray, "Lord, help!" From that point, everything seems to move in slow motion. The center hikes the ball to the holder. The ball spirals like a missile to the holder, who in one motion catches it and brings it down to the flat tee—spinning the ball to get the laces facing the goal. On that launch pad, the football stops spinning for a split second before my foot meets it. For a moment, I am one with the ball. I feel it bend around my foot, and with a thump it lifts off the tee and clears the line of scrimmage.

As I look up to follow the trajectory of the football, I know that I've hit it well, but quickly realize that I have pulled it a little to the left. To compensate, I lean hard to the right—hoping that by some invisible force I can coax the ball to correct itself in mid-flight. As the pigskin floats toward the goal, I notice that the ball is headed on a collision course with the left upright. I cringe watching the football spin in a backward motion—locked in on that goal post.

*Thoink.*

Careening off the left post, it flutters down toward the horizontal post and bounces. Like a dying quail, the ball flops over the goal post and falls to the ground. The kick is good! We win! My heart can start beating again.

That was the happy ending of a western Oklahoma, small town high school football game I played in the late 70's. No doubt, the celebration was sweet, and I got to be a hero. But looking back, I believe that the real hero was someone who didn't wear shoulder pads or don a jersey.

The moment before the kick will be forever etched in my mind. My coach put his arms on my shoulders, locked eyes with mine, and with a grin said, "Steve, you've made this a million times in practice. Stay loose, and just go out there and nail it." Then he spun me around and slapped me on the rear and sent me out on the field. My coach's "go-out-and-nail-it" way of thinking set me up for whatever success I experienced that night on the gridiron, and that same philosophy has served me well in dealing with other more weighty challenges since.

But let's contrast this "nail it" mentality with what I call "don't miss" motivation. Kickers get it all the time from fans and teammates who don't understand the dynamics of success. People often yell something like, "Hey Steve! We really need this kick, so don't miss!" Or, "We're all counting on you, so don't let us down." In football language, this is what you would call "icing the kicker." And believe me, it doesn't help. To threaten or implore a kicker to "not miss" is a bad set-up.

In fact, whatever negative image we are to avoid actually draws us to it. Parents understand this with their kids when they're having fun with reverse psychology. I really enjoyed warping my kids' minds when they were little. "Okay, Zach, whatever you do, *do not* eat this bite of broccoli. It's for me. I don't want you to have it. In fact, I'll be really sad if you (CHOMP!)...What?! You just ate my broccoli! You better not do that again!"

Why does reverse psychology often work on kids? The same reason it works on you and me. Whatever we focus on will draw us in. "Nail it" thinkers focus on positive results, not on negative possibilities. Athletes who excel demonstrate this all the time. Michael Jordan had a "nail it" mentality when he played basketball. When he took the last shot to win the game, he knew it was going in, and so did everyone else in the arena. More often than not, he nailed those crucial jumpers. How did he get so good? Well, those who played with him talk of his legendary work ethic—being the first on the floor for practice and the last to leave. They talk about his leadership and how he called for the best out of those around him. They talk about how he played entire games in his head, envisioning how he would respond and how he would overcome any adverse situation. By the time Michael Jordan stepped onto the basketball court, he was physically and mentally prepared like few who have ever played the game.

Tiger Woods is another athlete who demonstrates the "nail it" mentality. Granted, off the golf course, he's had his personal issues and character defects, but on the course he has amazing abilities. When his ball finds a rough lie in the middle of a stand of tall grass or behind some trees, he often comes up with incredible shots to keep him at the top of the leader board. How did he get so good at ad lib shots in tough situations? Tiger explains. "As a kid, I might have been psycho, I guess, but I used to throw golf balls in the trees and try and somehow make par from them. I thought that was fun."[1] Tiger focused on achieving positive results from any position on the golf course, and he had a good time practicing under the worst conditions.

As helpful as the "nail it" mentality is for athletes, I believe that it is of even greater value to those who face the challenges of life—which can sometimes loom much larger than a steel goal post or a tree in the middle of our fairway.

What you think about, and how you think about what you think about, can make you or break you. This applies to performance issues. It applies to contentment issues. It applies to relationship issues. And I want to demonstrate in this book that it applies to issues related to how we deal with suffering. Mark this down. Your life will only be meaningful and effective if you view the problem of suffering the way championship level sufferers have seen it.

And yes, boys and girls, there will be a test! What you believe about suffering will be tested in the crucible of your one and only life. Eventually, no matter who you are, you will face less than ideal circumstances. Eventually, disaster comes and we will come head to head with hardships of some kind or another. No one has to go looking for trouble or difficulties. In time, trouble finds us.

I believe that there is a "nail it" way to look at suffering—to be able to focus on the positive results and not on the negative possibilities. I believe that there is a way to face suffering that can help us do more than just outlast our tough times, but to actually be transformed by our tough times. If you will stick with me, and we keep walking together, I think you'll find help, strength, encouragement, wisdom, and maybe even a little bit of inspiration on the road to true transformation.

In a few chapters, I want to introduce you to one of the ultimate "nail it" thinkers of all time. But before I do that, I need to take you to the place where this "nail it" way of life I'd learned from my coach got severely tested. To tell you about it, let's hop on a Greyhound bus that will eventually stop in Lincoln, Nebraska. When we get there, you better get your helmet on and snap up your chin-strap. You never know what might happen when you aren't looking.

# Chapter Two: Now, Think On These Things...

*"Summing it all up, friends, I'd say you'll do best by filling your minds and meditating on things true, noble, reputable, authentic, compelling, gracious—the best, not the worst; the beautiful, not the ugly; things to praise, not things to curse. Put into practice what you learned from me, what you heard and saw and realized. Do that, and God, who makes everything work together, will work you into his most excellent harmonies."*
— The Apostle Paul, Philippians 4:4-9 (The Message)

After I finished high school, I began to pursue my dream of playing big-time college football. I turned down several scholarship opportunities at some small colleges so that I could walk-on at Oklahoma State University. Jimmy Johnson, who in later years became the coach of the Super Bowl champion Dallas Cowboys, was the coach at OSU. Then, he was known as a young coach on the rise. I identified with that, because I felt like I was on the rise. I just knew that I was going to be the next great OSU kicker—even if they couldn't find a scholarship for me right away.

In the fall of my freshman year, I had to sit out. There were seniors ahead of me, and I was told by the kicking coaches to keep practicing and then come back in the spring. I did, and during spring practices, I survived a meat grinder of drills that all the walk-ons went through to weed out those who didn't have any business playing at that level. Sometimes they'd send us out to be tackling dummies for the linebackers to practice their form tackling. On many occasions, after meeting up with a linebacker or two, I'd be looking through my ear-hole—staggering back to the line just in time to run another drill for another linebacker to knock me down again.

But my perseverance paid off. In the fall of my sophomore year, I made the junior varsity team and was on my way. While I didn't have a great shot in the field goal kicking department, I had moved up the depth charts for the punters and was pushing the starting punter.

I'll never forget the day when I got to put on the OSU jersey and run out on the field to play that first JV game. I knew it was the beginning of bigger and better things. My first game was in Kansas, and I got to punt. I did fairly well, averaging about 40 yards a punt.

The next week, we went to Nebraska to take on their fearsome freshman football squad. During that week of practice, I was in a zone. I had never punted so well. And one day, our starting punter was having an off day.

In one of the punting drills, Johnson got frustrated, and in an exasperated tone shouted, "I need somebody who can punt the blankety blank ball! Is there anybody who can punt around here?!"

My position coach hollered, "Reed! Get in there!"

I jumped in the huddle, and everyone looked at me like I was supposed to know what to say. So I asked, "Am I supposed to say something?"

One of my friends on the team said, "Just say 'spread punt on one.'"

"Okay guys, spread punt on one. Ready, break!"

I backed up 14 yards behind the center, and just like in high school, it seemed that it all happened in slow motion. I hollered, "Ready! Down! Set! Hut one!" And the football came zipping back to me. I caught the ball and in one fluid motion laid it on my foot and kicked it into a tight spiral that floated more than 50 yards in the air with good hang time. Johnson clapped his hands in front of my face and cheered, "That's the way to punt the ball! Let's do it again!" Five straight times, the result was the same. And the whole team was buzzing because I showed up the starter.

Two days later, I was on the team bus heading for Lincoln. If I showed my stuff against the feared Nebraska Cornhuskers, then I just might get a chance to move up. I could hardly wait for the game.

After a night of tossing and turning, I welcomed the chance to get up and join the team for breakfast, and then we headed for the stadium. In pre-game warm-ups, I was still in my zone—punting like I'd always dreamed I would.

After the opening kickoff, our offense got the ball. In typical fashion for that day, it was three plays and out. My first punt was decent, traveling about 35 yards, but nothing to write home about. My second punt was a little further, but it was low, giving the return man more time and space to run. Before I knew it, their guy was streaking down the sidelines with a convoy of three Nebraska bruisers escorting him down the field.

My first thought was, "Oh boy. Somebody better slow him down." My next thought was, "I think I am the last one between this wall of red and the goal line." As I tried to run alongside of this human shield and just stay out of the way (kickers are not known to be brave!), one of the Nebraska players caught up with me and hit me with a glancing blow to the shoulder—knocking me off my stride. I tried to put my left foot down to regain my balance, but in doing so, my left shoe got caught in the turf. In a split second that seemed to last an eternity, my body went somersaulting while my foot remained firmly stuck to the ground. In that moment, I felt my knee bend backwards in a grotesque, awkward way. Unbeknownst to me, I created a pile-up that actually allowed one of our guys to tackle their runner on the three yard line. The next play they scored. (So much for sacrificing for the team!)

From that day on, my knee and my life would never be the same. That little episode started me on a yearlong process involving surgery, rehab, and physical therapy to seek to regain what I'd lost on that field in Lincoln, Nebraska. My knee never fully recovered, and my football career was finished.

Right after my injury, I tried to go back and look at the film, but the coaches wouldn't allow me to see it. Years later, I learned that my injury (and several other injuries on our team in that game) prompted the end of playing JV games against Nebraska during that era of Nebraska football. Nebraska just had too many bodies in comparison to our smaller squads—and could literally mow down teams that were trying to build for the future.

During this time, I was heavily involved in church and student ministries on campus. So it was natural for some of my Christian friends to come by to cheer me up. A couple of times, one of them would ask something like, "Steve, do you think God's trying to tell you something here?" Their implication was that God was punishing me for a secret sin or that maybe He didn't want me playing football anymore, so He caused my injury, knowing that I would be able to spend more time doing campus ministry. As you might imagine, that didn't sit too well with me at the time.

My answer to my friends is one that still makes sense to me today. I said something like this, "I believe that sometimes things simply happen because we step out onto the playing fields of life. When I stepped out on that artificial turf in Nebraska, there was a chance (even though it might be more remote for a kicker) that I'd get injured. That's simply the game of football, and I don't think God did this to me to set me straight over something." As I reflected more in moments alone with God, I was convinced that God *allowed* me to suffer, but that He didn't do it to whack me for a secret sin or for taking a wayward path. Though I was still a card carrying sinner like everyone else, this suffering seemed different. I held tight to Romans 8:28, a verse that says...

> *And we know that in all things God works for the good of those who love him, who are called according to his purpose.*

In faith I just had to believe that God would somehow use my pain to make me what He wanted me to become. In spite of my circumstances, I really wanted to believe.

Looking back, I can see how wrestling with this issue at a relatively young age put me on a lifelong quest to pay attention to how people view and respond to suffering and tragedy. And this experience sent me looking to the scriptures to try to make sense of it all. It didn't take long for one of my heroes of the Bible to stand out to me. His name? The Apostle Paul. Paul was a great missionary and the author of the above verse of scripture.

I was drawn to him initially because of his physical ailment—what Paul called his "thorn in the flesh" that plagued him. According to the scriptures, on three occasions, Paul begged God to take away his thorn. And each time he was rejected. The last time God simply said, "My grace is enough for you."

Paul helped me see that suffering and sin are not necessarily one-to-one correlations. If anyone deserved a healing from his suffering, it would be Paul. Paul was a great man. But God didn't take away all of his physical problems. For some reason, God chose *not* to grant Paul his healing.

As I looked at how Paul came to terms with his pain and lived his life completely devoted to God, he became one of my models for coming to peace with my physical ailment and moving on with my life.

How did Paul do it? Well, for one, he thought differently. Paul wrote the words to the scripture passage we read at the beginning of this chapter. And what did he say? He told us to think about the good stuff, to have a joyful heart, to pray instead of worry. He implored us to think about the noble things, the right things, the pure things, the admirable things, the excellent things, the beautiful things. In Paul's own way he coached us to have a "nail it" mentality even when facing very difficult circumstances.

Paul knew the importance of focusing on the positive. But this was a lot bigger and a lot more profound than a speech about the power of positive thinking. After all, he penned these words from behind bars—in a prison cell! Apparently, Paul knew a secret about handling tough times that few ever get a chance to know and experience. Where did he come up with this?

When we go back and trace Paul's steps, we see that he didn't exactly start off his life and ministry as a very positive person. In fact, he started off as one of the worst "don't miss" kind of guys you'd ever meet. Before Paul was "Paul-the-Christian," he was called by his Jewish name of "Saul." In Christian circles he was known as "Saul-the-persecutor-of-Christians." He was a religious zealot who was so intent on keeping Judaism pure and undefiled, that he did so by linking up with a group that actually hunted down and killed Christians. (Talk about a real "killjoy!") Saul was there, holding the cloaks of the stone throwers who ripped them off to be better able to hurl the stones at Stephen—the first Christian martyr.

But later, Saul changed. Something happened, and he became one of the most profound "nail it" thinkers of his day. What was it that changed him?

Before we look at how he changed, let's meet up with Paul on one of his adventures. Let's travel back in time to a place where Paul is chained up inside one of his many prison cells. This one is in Philippi. As we go from the bright sunlight into the dark, dank dungeon, listen closely; you just might hear Paul singing with one of his jail buddies.

Oh, and one more thing. You might want to tip-toe. The guards have not been in a very good mood lately! Let's go.

# Chapter Three: Singing In Jail

*The warden threw a party in the county jail.*
*The prison band was there and they began to wail.*
*The band was jumpin' and the joint began to swing.*
*You should've heard those knocked out jailbirds sing.*
*Let's rock, everybody, let's rock.*
*Everybody in the whole cell block*
*Was dancin' to the jailhouse rock.[1]*
　　　　　　　—Elvis Presley singing *Jailhouse Rock*

"Who is that girl?"

"She is a slave. She has a special ability where she can tell fortunes—making her masters a lot of money. Whoops. I think she saw us! She's coming over now to talk to Paul and Silas."

"These men are servants of the Most High God!" she screamed in a demonic craze. "They are telling you how you can be saved!"

Paul and his companions were on their way to a prayer meeting with other believers, and apparently this same scene had been repeated over many days. This time, however, Paul was so bothered by the situation that instead of saying his usual nice words to her, he turned and ordered the spirit, "By the power of Jesus Christ, I command you to come out of her!" Immediately, the spirit came out, and the girl went limp. No longer was there a crazed look in her eyes, and she walked over to talk more with Paul and Silas.

When the owners of the slave girl saw this, they realized that she didn't have her powers anymore, and that they could not use her to make money. "Get them!" they yelled. So they grabbed Paul and Silas and dragged them before the city rulers in the marketplace. "These men are Jews and are making trouble in our city!" they accused indignantly. "They are teaching things that are not right for us as Romans to do!"

As their complaints grew louder, a crowd joined to attack them. Soon, the Roman officers tore the clothes off the backs of Paul and Silas and had them beaten with rods. Battered, bruised, and bleeding, they were then ushered over to the prison and thrown in jail. The jailer was ordered to guard them carefully, so he put them far inside the prison and pinned their feet down between large blocks of wood. About midnight, Paul and Silas began to sing and pray. As they sang praises to God, the other prisoners must have wondered who these men were. Perhaps they talked to one another through the walls. Suddenly, the earth began to roll, and a terrifying earthquake shook the foundations of the jail. The doors broke open, and all the prisoners were freed from their chains. The jailer woke up and saw the open doors. He knew by Roman law that he would die if he lost his prisoners. Thinking that the prisoners had already escaped, he drew his sword and was about to thrust it into his heart.

"Don't do it!" Paul shouted. "We're all here!"

The jailer called out to someone to bring a torch. Then he ran inside and, shaking with fear, fell down before Paul and Silas. He brought them outside and implored, "What must I do to be saved?"

"Believe in the Lord Jesus, and you will be saved," they answered. "And the same is true for you and all the people in your house." At that revelation, a grateful jailer took Paul and Silas to his home located a short distance away. He washed their wounds and fed them as they shared their faith. With glad hearts the jailer and everyone in the house wanted to be baptized immediately. After Paul and Silas baptized them, joy filled the hearts of all, because God had shown up, and they all believed in Jesus. (This is a retelling of the biblical story from Acts 16:1-34).

\*\*\*\*\*\*\*\*\*\*\*\*\*\*\*\*\*\*\*\*\*\*\*\*\*\*\*\*\*\*\*\*\*\*\*\*\*\*\*\*\*\*\*\*\*\*\*\*\*\*\*\*\*\*\*\*\*\*\*\*\*\*\*\*\*\*\*\*\*\*\*\*\*\*\*\*\*\*\*\*\*\*\*

One of my claims to fame is that I lived two doors down from Garth Brooks in the jock dorm at Oklahoma State University. Few people today know that Garth was a javelin thrower in college. But in the days I knew him, that was the most important part of his identity. Sure, Garth strummed a guitar in his dorm room, but none of us would have predicted that our buddy would one day become the mega-star that he is today.

When I think about Garth, I remember a fun-loving, curly-headed guy with a lot of dreams. I also remember his way of denying the reality of his athletic abilities. At the time, I thought he needed to get a grip. Now, in hindsight, I can see that Garth's ability to deny reality actually came in handy when he had to face so much rejection during the days he chased his dream of making it big in the country music business. But consider this. When it came to making music, was Garth really denying reality? Looking back, he *wasn't* in denial, he was more in touch with reality than anyone could have imagined.

To be sure, Garth had to sing his way through some tough times, waiting for his big break to come. If there is one thing I admire most about Garth, it is his ability to keep singing even when times are tough. In a similar vein, singing through difficult days is the hallmark of many great people. And what we read about Paul and Silas singing in jail makes me stop and take notice of the character of these men.

Would you have sung if you had been beaten and thrown in that jail? All musical talent aside, the mere notion of singing in jail would probably be about the furthest thing from our minds and our lips. But here we find Paul and his buddy Silas singing their famous "jailhouse rock" long before Elvis ever came along. And apparently, they weren't singing the blues. The scripture tells us that these songs arose out of their prayers, and it appears that these songs expressed praise and thanksgiving to God. They were singing out of joy! Unbelievable!!

What might have prepared these men for this moment? Were they delusional? Were they enamored with jail ministry? Were they just more spiritual than most? I believe the answer to that question can be found in Paul's conversion and call to ministry.

When Paul was known as Saul, he was on an assignment to locate some Christians in Damascus and bring them back as prisoners to Jerusalem. On the road to Damascus, Paul was blinded by a bright light. And Jesus Himself asked him, "Saul, Saul! Why are you persecuting Me?" A conversation followed, and Saul was led to Damascus.

Meanwhile, in Damascus, a follower of Jesus was having his own encounter with the Lord. The Lord spoke to Ananias in a dream and told him to go to the place where he would find a "Saul of Tarsus" and have the opportunity to lay hands on Saul and restore his sight. But Ananias had heard about Saul's murderous plots against those who were following Jesus, and he pointed that out to God. But the Lord told Ananias,

> "Go! This man is my chosen instrument to carry my name before the Gentiles and their kings and before the people of Israel. I will show him how much he must suffer for my name." Acts 9:15-16

The Bible tells us that Ananias did go lay hands on Saul, and his sight was restored. And presumably, Ananias told him what God wanted to do with him—that he would be a missionary to the Gentiles, that he would appear before kings, that he would speak to the people of Israel, and (here's the kicker) that God Himself would show him how much he would have to suffer for the cause.

This last phrase, I've dubbed "the suffering clause." It's the fine print to Paul's conversion experience and his call to ministry. God Himself promises to show Paul how much he will suffer for the cause of Christ. He won't understand it in that moment, but God will show it to him along the way.

So, fast forward many years to when Paul, the Christian, is hanging on to a plank in the middle of the Mediterranean Sea, what must he be thinking? I believe he's thinking, "This shipwreck must be part of that 'suffering clause' that God told me about. So I guess I'll hang on."

When Paul is groggily coming to after being nearly stoned to death and left for dead, what is he thinking? Again, I surmise that he's thinking, "This must be part of the suffering God told me to expect. I'm alive, so with God's help and the help of my friends, I will dust myself off and head to the next town."

When he is tormented by his thorn in the flesh and wonders if he will ever be relieved of this pain, what goes through his head? I believe he's thinking, "This must be a part of the suffering that Ananias told me was part of my calling as a follower of Jesus. So I suppose I'd better keep on doing what I can with the strength God has given me for today." I wonder if this is what gave Paul the ability to one day write to the Philippian church and say,

*"I have learned to be content whatever the circumstances."*
*Philippians 4:11*

Through the years, Paul had "learned" to be content. It didn't come automatically. This ability came through experience. Paul had to learn it by living it.

So in time, he could honestly say that whether he was well fed or hungry or living with plenty or in need—he could be content. How? I believe it came in coming to terms with the "suffering clause." And this coming to terms with suffering is something that I believe is not just unique to Paul. I believe, after searching the scriptures and comparing notes with Christians all over the world, that this clause comes in the fine print of every conversion of every Christian and in the fine print of every call of every church leader. And more significantly, I believe that it is this "suffering clause" that is at the heart of Paul's secret to being content in all circumstances.

For us, it can become one biblical truth that not only helps us *survive* in life and ministry, but also becomes something that can help us *thrive* in life and ministry. As we see our circumstances from God's eternal perspective, we can hang on to the fact that whatever we face right now is not the last word on our lives. God still holds all the trump cards and can take our temporary troubles and transform them in ways we can't even imagine in our own understanding.

This can be seen graphically in the annals of church history and in the amazing stories of current day revivals and people movements. Later in the book, I'll share a few examples of some of these movements where believers have suffered well and been beacons of hope to other people who observed their loving and courageous ways of dealing with adversity.

For some reason, God has chosen to use this suffering clause as a way to prepare His people from all walks of life for increased ministry effectiveness to hurting people. When people get in touch with their suffering clause, it frees them up to live a courageous and contagious

Christian lifestyle. And occasionally, this gets played out in arenas that prompt hundreds of thousands of people to come to Christ. Paul certainly got to experience a full range of this in his life and ministry.

So now, with this information, why do you think Paul and Silas sang in jail? If you're buying what I'm saying, you know it has something to do with this "suffering clause." In this instance, it can be traced. Before these men were thrown in jail, both of them had seen God do some amazing things. They knew God was going to get the last word. They'd seen Him work in many places they'd already been. Just that day, they'd experienced the exhilaration of God using them to turn a slave girl's life around. So even though they were beaten and hurting, they knew that every stripe was for the cause of Christ. So they rejoiced. And in those dark moments in a jail cell, they instinctively—if not intentionally, prayed and praised God.

Undoubtedly their prayers and their praises affected the other prisoners—so much so that after the earthquake shook, and all could have escaped the jail, they didn't. Have you thought about that miracle? A prisoner who doesn't get the heck out of Dodge is either stupid or held back by something powerfully attractive. And that miracle of the "un-escaped" prisoners led to the miraculous conversion of the jailer, who would have most likely been executed at a later time for losing prisoners on his watch.

So the jailer welcomed Paul and Silas into his home, and his whole family came to Christ, which had to have encouraged the budding church in Philippi that was meeting in the home of a business woman named Lydia. Perhaps the jailer's home became a new house church and served to help multiply other house churches in the region. Because the believers in Philippi got a special letter from Paul that made it into our Bible, we can surmise that significant growth took place there—all in the middle of very trying circumstances.

The suffering clause. It's something else. And I am convinced that when we embrace it and get in touch with it, we stand in the strongest position possible for ultimate transformation to take place.

Now, I know that the discerning reader may still wonder how getting in touch with the "suffering clause" truly fits into the "nail it" way of thinking that I advocated in the beginning of the book. We're getting closer to the heart of this but haven't gotten to the real zinger yet. So, walk with me a few more chapters, and know that when we get to the ultimate answer, I'll hire a marching band to make a lot of noise to make sure that you're awake at that point!

Before I start getting out my wallet, I want to tell you about a Focus on the Family broadcast I heard while I was writing this book. On that day, Dr. James Dobson interviewed Dayna Curry and Heather Mercer—two of the relief workers in Afghanistan who were held captive with several others from various countries because they had shown the *Jesus* movie. They told Dr. Dobson's audience that they loved to sing during those days of Taliban captivity. Spontaneously, Dr. Dobson asked them to sing one of their songs—which they did. And I've got to tell you, I got chills as they sang one of the songs that brought them comfort while they were imprisoned. There was a depth of heart that came pouring out as they sang—even a higher purity of soul that just rang out in their melody. As I leaned in to listen to my radio, I wanted what they had.

If you were to ask them, "Do you want to go back to that prison under those conditions again?" I'd suppose they'd say "no." They desperately wanted to go home during those days. But would they speak of a kind of joy that they experienced there? Absolutely. In fact, hours after they were freed, President Bush called them, and he sensed it. On the back cover of their book *Prisoners of Hope* the president is quoted saying, "...I sensed no bitterness in their voices, no fatigue, just joy. It was an uplifting experience for me to talk to these courageous souls."

No doubt, these girls got in touch with their suffering clause. And they'll never be the same. While my life hasn't had the same drama that they've experienced, I can certainly join them and say that getting in touch with my suffering clause has become one of the greatest things that ever happened to me. It didn't happen overnight, and I had to live through some tough times for many years before I understood the positive ramifications of what God was doing in my life.

My next stop in learning something about the suffering clause came about eight or nine years after my knee injury in Nebraska. This time, I'll need to take you to a small lake in the suburbs of Chicago. You might want to bring a jacket. It can get pretty chilly when the sun goes down in the upper Midwest.

# Chapter Four: My Suffering Clause

*"And we know that in all things God works for the good of those who love him, who are called according to his purpose."*
— The Apostle Paul, Romans 8:28

In spite of the disappointment of my football career ending, my college days turned into some of the most fun and meaningful days of my life. I got very involved in my church as we reached out each semester to hundreds of other college students. In addition to that, I spent a couple of years as a student assistant in the athletic dorm. And eventually I met the woman I'd get to marry. During those days it became clear that I wanted to pursue full time ministry after college graduation.

So, I got married and headed to Fort Worth, Texas, to attend seminary training for pastors. During seminary days, I became enamored with the idea that starting churches was one of the highest callings a minister could ever have. It took some time to convince Nola, my bride, but after hearing Rick Warren, author of *The Purpose Driven Life*, speak at a banquet about starting Saddleback Church (today one of the largest churches in the U.S.), we knew that our lives would involve the starting of churches in strategic places.

After completing my degree program, I figured that I was finally ready to start a church. Doors didn't open quickly, so I decided to do a Johnny Appleseed kind of church start—starting an English-speaking Hispanic church near where we lived in Fort Worth. Because part of my childhood years were spent in Costa Rica and Peru, I could speak Spanish and relate fairly well to the Hispanic culture. After starting the church, I turned it over to a Hispanic pastor and was ready to move on to my next assignment.

After much anticipation, we wound up in a suburb of Kansas City to start a church. From the beginning, we wanted that church to be a beacon to those who didn't go to church in our area. And anything I could get my hands on that would help me learn how to do that was latched onto, eaten up, and digested as quickly as possible. Not long after starting our new work, one of my pastor buddies told me about this amazing church up near Chicago that I just had to go see. So, without knowing a lot about it, I booked a flight and headed to a church leadership conference at Willow Creek Community Church.

The first time I stepped onto the campus, it felt like I was coming home. My whole life, I'd dreamed of a place like Willow, where people would become so contagious in their faith in Jesus that thousands would be touched over a short period of time. As I experienced the church for myself, I was forever hooked. After spending a couple of days there, I was so moved I could hardly stay in my seat. On that unforgettable morning in May, I put on my jacket and stepped out of the conference to take a walk. As I strolled around the lake on Willow's beautifully landscaped campus, Canadian geese were waddling around, some with fuzzy tennis ball goslings in tow. Birds were chirping in the trees. As I walked and prayed, there was a point when I looked up to heaven and asked, "God, would you bring this to our city?"

As I prayed that prayer, I wasn't praying for beautiful buildings or a pretty lake. I was praying that God would bring a church with a heart like the Willow Creek church to our region of Kansas City. As I waited on God for an answer, I walked a little further around the rim of the lake. And then, it was like God just stopped me in my tracks.

In my heart God said, "Yes, you will get to see this, but it will require more sacrifice than you can ever imagine at this time."

Not having any idea what I was saying, I gushed, "Then bring it on, Lord! I'm willing!"

In a moment that is now frozen in time, I believe I received my suffering clause—that I'd get to see something big happen in Kansas City, but that it would require more sacrifice than I could know.

Since that day, God has given me many occasions to discover the realities of that encounter with Him. I've gone back to that moment again and again, sometimes wondering if I just thought I heard from God, and sometimes resolutely believing that I was on track to experience God's plan for my life.

In those days, I hadn't discovered this "suffering clause" idea. I think at that time, I unconsciously believed that if I did everything right I'd experience success and a blessing from God. I'd get to be a super-star pastor and live happily ever after. Sure it would be tough, but we'd get to see our charts display lines that tracked mostly up and to the right.

It probably wouldn't surprise you if I said that I still had a thing or two to learn. Yet, as I look back on it, that prayer exchange with God became a stake in the ground that I've gone back to many times. It has become a source of both agony and ecstasy for me as I've tried to be faithful to God's leading in my life since that pivotal day by the lake. And though I didn't understand it at the time, my suffering clause was what kept me in ministry way past when I might have quit otherwise.

Looking back now, I'd go so far as to say that getting in touch with my suffering clause has become one of the greatest things that ever happened to me. It certainly helped sustain me during some of the storms that have blown my way—especially in the last few years.

But getting to this point didn't come quickly for me. I had to go through some suffering that I brought on myself first. In less than two years from my epiphany by the lake, the starry-eyed kid just out of seminary learned a very hard lesson that took the glitter and shine from the dream of creating a seeker targeted church in the suburbs of Kansas City—it wasn't pretty.

# Chapter Five: A Workaholic for God

*Six days you shall labor and do all your work, but the seventh day is a Sabbath to the LORD your God. On it you shall not do any work...* Exodus 20:9-10

When we started our first church, we got off to a great start. After about a year or so, we wound up on the front page of the metropolitan newspaper, the *Kansas City Star*. In my mind, we had arrived and were now on our way to building a great church. In those days, it seemed that I had endless energy. And virtually everything we did, I made happen on sheer grit and hard work. In those days it was not unusual for me to go to bed at 10:30 or 11:00 p.m., wake at 3 a.m. and work a few hours, and then catnap before Nola got up to go to work. Then I'd put in a "normal" day of work like everyone else. The net result was not good. I was routinely putting in 60-70 hours a week while trying to be vigilant in being there for my wife and 2-year-old little boy.

About two years into the church start, I started feeling tired. But any time I cut back on my hours at church, it would be noticeable, and I'd suck it up and strive to work harder.

One day I was pounding away on the computer, writing my sermon for the following Sunday. In a moment of sheer exhaustion, I fell asleep with my head on the keyboard. When I woke up, I saw a bunch of gobbledygook on the screen, looked at my watch, and figured I must have been asleep for about 3 hours! In that moment, my insanity slapped me in the face. I was a certifiable mess, and my slobbery keyboard both grossed me out and scared me half to death. I was out of control and didn't know what to do about it.

I'd heard about AA (Alcoholics Anonymous), and that their 12 step program had been applied to addictions of all kinds. So in an act of desperation, I got the AA "Big Book" and decided to try applying the 12 steps to my problem.

In the coming months I became a closet 12-stepper. And with each step I took, I regained a little more health and perspective in my life. I cut the hours I was working for the church to 50-55 per week. But as my personal life got in order, the church suffered. When I cut my hours, the church declined, partly because I had unwittingly designed it around what I could personally do. When I let go of some things, and no one else came along to take up the slack, we lost momentum.

So, in spite of our great start, by the third year we had dwindled in our attendance and, after months of agonizing, decided to close down the church of my dreams. In those days, I often asked God, "Lord, did I get my wires crossed by the lake at Willow?" Yet over and over I heard, "This will require more sacrifice than you can imagine."

For the next year, our family attended another church in the area—figuring that our dream would have to be realized by someone else. We needed a break, so I started a business in my garage shredding confidential documents for companies, and we decided to be regular church folks.

The church that welcomed us was a true God-send to us. They loved us and gave us time to rest and heal from the battle wounds we'd suffered. At one point I figured that maybe God wanted me to be the best Christian businessman I could be. But that didn't last long. For me, the call to ministry was too strong. There were nights when I'd wake up in the middle of the night with what I thought was a great idea for a sermon. I'd be feverishly writing away on it for an hour or so and then realize, "I don't have anyone to share this with. I'm writing this for nobody! I must be nuts!" Then I'd go back to bed. During those days, I couldn't help but write about the lessons I'd learned and about why our church didn't make it. I sought to redeem the time in healing and reflection.

But after about a year of bench time, I realized that my business was not where my heart was. I had to get back into the calling that I loved. Thankfully, Nola didn't quench my renewed call to ministry. Even though she would have been happy if we had stayed in our roles in the wonderful church we had been attending, she saw that I was craving more ministry action and was willing to make major adjustments for me to be able to do what I felt God created me to do.

It was at that point that Rick McGinniss, a friend of mine who was starting a church in the northern suburbs of Kansas City, Missouri, called me and eventually asked me to join his team to start North Heartland Community Church. During the start-up of North Heartland, Rick regularly pulled from my quiver of lessons learned and validated me at a time when I was still a little gun-shy from our past church-starting disappointment. Amazingly, North Heartland took off like a rocket and soon was averaging over 300 people each week in the middle school where we held services. Now, over 15 years later, they are one of the strongest churches in that region—doing a great job at reaching out to the unchurched.

But as good as North Heartland was for us, there came a point where we felt that God wanted us to try again in Johnson County, Kansas—our first church-starting location. After a couple of years at North Heartland, we were sent off with their blessing to start another congregation.

Because of my earlier experience, I had sworn off Lone Ranger style church planting forever. This time, I was more patient in pulling the trigger—waiting until we had a die-hard team to serve as a leadership nucleus before making it public that we were starting. Before launching the church, I met a guy who became a good friend who was also looking to start a church in the same area. Despite some cautions from some of our friends, we decided to be co-pastors of this new start. In addition, we gathered a staff team to complement our gifts and stepped out in faith.

Like North Heartland, this one took off. Without seeking the media out, within the first couple of months, a reporter found us, and we wound up on the front page of the *Kansas City Star*. Sound familiar? Even with some bumps along the way, in a couple of years, we had a dedicated core of 150-180 people regularly coming to services in a junior high school. And on good Sundays we were more than 200 strong. Life was good.

I reveled in the thought that this church was the one that God promised by the lake at Willow. It *had* required more sacrifice than I could imagine. But we were on our way. Nothing could stop it from happening now, could it?

# Chapter Six: Praying Dangerous Prayers

*Are any among you suffering? They should keep on praying about it.*
James 5:13 (New Living Translation)

"Prayer does not equip us for greater works. Prayer *is* the greater work."[1] —Oswald Chambers

Have you ever prayed a dangerous prayer? If you've ever prayed for patience, you know what I mean! If you pray for patience, what does God give you? He'll give you a frustrating situation to practice your patience!

I don't recall the first time I heard about this concept of praying dangerous prayers (though I had unwittingly been doing it on occasion), but several years ago, I heard the phrase and the concept. The idea is a little more involved than praying for things like patience, but it is still pretty simple. A dangerous prayer is a costly prayer that would revolutionize my spiritual life if God answered it. In a way, my prayer at Willow fit that category. "Lord, bring this to our city."

In July of 1999, I had just finished reading Rory Noland's book *The Heart of an Artist*. In it, he mentioned the dangerous prayer concept—stating that he had a dangerous prayer he tried to pray each year. As I read that, it challenged me to consider doing that for the coming year. So I took off on a walk to ponder what an appropriate prayer would be for me.

To explain how this happened, I'll need to give you a peek into my prayer life. You've already seen hints of it in this book. Years ago, I gave up on the traditional, quiet-time, praying-in-a-closet style of journaling and praying. It just seemed more like a duty, and over the years I had discovered that some of my greatest times in prayer were spent out in nature. And more specifically, these were times spent walking in nature.

So, because we live in a home that backs up to a park, most mornings I get up and walk in the park and pray. Hence, my "walk with God" is a literal "walk with God." As I walk, I simply pray, "Lord, what is the one thing you want me to do today?" I don't ask for a long list of things. I'm more interested in honing in on one thing. Then, for the rest of the day, I attempt to follow through on whatever God impresses me to do. When I get back to the house, if there's something that strikes me on the walk that needs to be written about, I write about it, or I take action that is appropriate to the leading I get for the day.

Well, on that day in July when I was pondering what would be appropriate for me to claim as a dangerous prayer for the year, I had been studying a passage in the first chapter of the book of Acts. The passage depicts a time after Jesus was raised from the dead. Jesus had already made several post-resurrection appearances. And one of the last things He told his followers before ascending into heaven is found in Acts 1:8. On this day, Jesus' words just plain captured me.

> "But you will receive power when the Holy Spirit comes upon you; and you will be my witnesses in Jerusalem, and in all Judea and Samaria, and to the ends of the earth."

As I walked, I thought about how Jesus wanted those disciples to focus first on where they were—in Jerusalem. From there, they would share the message of Christ in Judea—the surrounding region. Then it would go to Samaria—a place on the other side of the tracks with people very different from them. And ultimately, they would be called to get the message out to the whole world.

Then I got to thinking about me. If I were to see this happen in my life, what would it look like? Where was my Jerusalem? It was right there, in Johnson County, Kansas. And as I mentioned before, my Jerusalem ministry was going well.

Then I thought about my Judea—our surrounding region—Kansas City. I wondered how God might use me in a wider area.

I thought about Samaria—the other side of the tracks. I wondered what God might want to do with me in places with people who weren't like me.

And then I thought about faraway places, ends-of-the-earth kinds of places. I thought about places I'd been when I was a kid when my parents were missionaries in Costa Rica and Peru. With each step, a prayer was forming in my heart. I realized that more than anything, I wanted to be a witness for Christ in each of these places—in my Jerusalem, Judea, Samaria, and to the ends of the earth.

So in the middle of that walk, I prayed my dangerous prayer for the year. "Lord, make me Your witness." When I got back from my walk, I wanted to mark the moment, so I pulled out this big yellow note card and wrote the whole thing out.

*"July 17, 1999… My dangerous prayer and verse… Lord, make me Your witness. Acts 1:8"*

I then pinned the card to my bulletin board in my office and forgot about it. A few weeks later, in dealing with a conflict in the church, my co-pastor friend hit me with a bombshell. He said that he felt that God was calling him to be senior pastor of our church. At first I thought he was joking, and I slapped my knee and said, "That's a good one!" But he wasn't joking. And that set in motion a bizarre set of circumstances that prompted me in September—September 12, 1999—to resign from the church that I loved more than words can express.

During the days that followed, my walk in the mornings became my primary means of emotional survival. In fact, there were times I'd wake up in the wee hours of the morning and walk in the pitch black darkness. Sometimes, I'd walk for a couple of hours until the sun would dawn. Those were truly some rough days and nights. And, believe me, I went to God over and over with the question, "Is this more of the sacrifice that I'd understand later? God, I thought we were done!"

During those dark days, I made a decision that helped me survive. I decided that I wasn't going to try to figure it all out in that moment. I decided that I'd just bask in the presence of God. So, I literally spent hours in unhurried walks with God. As I walked, I poured out my emotions. And each day, I felt ambushed by His grace and mercy. Every day God met me in a way that I can hardly tell you about without getting choked up. The times with God were so rich and so sweet, that even to this day I can't help but feel a sense of gratitude for that time. It's hard to explain, but the reality for me was that even during the worst of those days, God was so incredibly close to me. Yes, I was painfully aware that my whole life and identity had been stripped from me. Still, there was that unmistakable and reassuring presence of God that was so meaningful each day.

I now possessed a secret weapon that no one could take away from me. I felt that I had something deep inside that helped me love people better. I realized God really could help me handle more than I'd ever dreamed I could and that even in the worst of it, I could still flourish in my soul. I now sensed that I had an advantage. And in moments of what some would deem insanity, I almost pitied those who hadn't experienced what I'd gone through!

In October, my parents told me that they were going to Costa Rica in January for a 10-day mission project. Costa Rica was where we lived for a year when I was 9 years old. They asked if I wanted to go. Knowing that I might need the cash to pay for the trip, Dad added that if I painted their house, he'd pay my way. I thought about it and realized that I didn't have anything better to do, so I said, "Sure!" I painted their house and began to prepare for the trip.

Just a few weeks before heading to Costa Rica, a minister from another church, who heads up her church's prayer ministry, gave me an Oswald Chambers quote that stuck with me. You read it at the beginning of this chapter. "Prayer does not equip us for greater works. Prayer *is* the greater work."

I spent many a walk pondering that phrase—wondering if I really understood it. It seemed right. I wondered if up until that point I'd gotten my ministry priorities in reverse. I'd come up with the plans and then in prayer would ask God to bless those plans.

So I decided to take a chance on a new pattern of ministry for me. I didn't have a church, so I had nothing to lose. I decided that I would let whatever ministry God might give me flow out of my prayer life and nothing else. I decided that I'd take a walk each day and simply do what God wanted me to do for that day—nothing more, and nothing less.

Little did I know that this combination of Costa Rica, a dangerous prayer, and an Oswald Chambers' quote would forever change my life. I think it all gets captured in one day in Costa Rica.

# Chapter Seven: The Ministry of Tears

*Those who sow in tears will reap with songs of joy. He who goes out weeping, carrying seed to sow, will return with songs of joy, carrying sheaves with him.* Psalm 126:5-6

*"Blessed are those who mourn for they will be comforted."*
— Jesus, Matthew 5:4

Prior to our arrival in Costa Rica, many churches there had been doing what they called "Operation Andrew." It was a prayer emphasis based on the example of the disciple Andrew, who brought his brother Peter to Jesus. I have since learned that Billy Graham's organization used this strategy of prayer when they prepared cities for their crusades. But it was all new to me. They had encouraged the participants in the crusade to write down the names of 10 of their friends and family who didn't know Christ. And each day they prayed for these people. For nine months, many had been praying fervently for those on their "Operation Andrew" lists.

Meanwhile many of us from all over the world prepared to converge on Costa Rica for this 10-day project. Once we arrived, we split up to work in individual churches from coast to coast. On my team, there were 10 of us from various countries who came to work in a church near a university campus in the capital city of San José. The group consisted of two of us from the States, one from Guatemala, two from Honduras, a couple from Nicaragua, one from Panama, one from Chile, and one from El Salvador. Each day the people from the church set up visits for us to go and meet as many of the people on their prayer lists as they could set up. In each visit we'd simply go to help them figure out where they stood in their relationship to Christ. That method of visiting people on those "Operation Andrew" lists proved highly effective. Most of the people who gave their lives to Christ during that campaign did so on those visits. And then at night, we'd hold services in the church.

One day during that week stands out for me. We began in the morning with a visit with a middle-aged woman who worked in an upscale mall in San José. She managed a little flower shop on the third or fourth floor. As we walked into her colorful and cheerfully decorated store, we introduced ourselves, and after a moment of pleasantries, she invited us to a back room where we could sit and talk. She opened right up to us. Her eyes welled up, and with a quiver in her voice she told us that she was grieving the loss of her 32 year-old son who died the month before.

As soon as she said that, something about it just struck a chord within me. The rest of our team already knew this fact about her going into the visit, but for some reason I hadn't gotten the memo. So I was reacting more on instinct than anything. When she told us of her hurt, a tear came out of the corner of her eye and began to run down her cheek. As I noticed that tear, a tear crept out of the corner of my eye and slid down my face.

When she saw me tearing up, she let loose one on her other cheek. In sympathy, I matched her tear with one on the other side of my cheek, too! Within minutes, I was holding hands with this woman, and we were just sitting there crying together.

About that time, a couple of guys on our team, one from Guatemala, and the other from Costa Rica, said, "Esteban ("Steven" in Spanish), it looks like you have a lot to talk about. We're going to go out and walk around the mall for a bit…see ya later; bye!" And they were gone! So at this point, it was me, this woman, and Emelda—a woman on our team from Panama.

Where did the tears come from? For me the tears were driven by my thoughts of my brother-in-law, Richard. It had been about two and a half years since he died from cancer at the age of 38. I couldn't help but think of him. So I could identify with this woman's grief—not in words, but in tears. We cried for a few minutes. Then we talked about her relationship with Christ. She was a Catholic who had trusted in Jesus, but she really needed a support group to pray with and to be encouraged. So we talked about that, arranged for her to meet with some others from the church, and then excused ourselves after a good visit.

When I entered back into the flow of the mall, I was trying to wipe off the tears. But my emotions were still close to the surface. Emelda and I then began to look for the others. But we couldn't find them, so we decided to go to the first floor and see if they were waiting downstairs. We stepped into an elevator, and shortly before the doors closed, a young, attractive woman in her 20's slid in with us. She stood next to Emelda.

While we were going down, Emelda handed her a tract. I saw the exchange but barely noticed it, because I was still trying to hold myself together emotionally. When we got to the first floor, we looked around and couldn't find our team. We did find one of the men, so we decided that instead of running around in a wild goose chase looking for the others, we'd send this one guy to do the searching while Emelda and I waited on a park bench out in front. We walked outside and sat on this bench.

As we did so, we hadn't noticed that this young woman from the elevator had been following us. When we sat down, I looked up just in time to see her simultaneously walking and reading our tract—and walking toward us! When she got near us, she sat down on our bench next to Emelda. Emelda turned to her and asked, "Have you read it?"

"Yes," she said. "But I don't understand it."

"You want me to explain it to you?"

"Please do."

In the next few moments, Emelda explained how a person could pray a prayer to receive God's gift of salvation. As she did that, tears just started welling up in me. I could see what was about to happen! And the joy produced tears that I didn't know what to do with. At one point, I looked at this Costa Rican woman and felt that I needed to explain why I was crying, so I began my complicated explanation.

"I'm a little sad because upstairs there's this woman who lost her 32 year-old son last month, and it reminds me of my brother-in-law."

I was about to go on when she gave me a look that spoke volumes to me. She didn't say anything, but her look said, "Steve, you don't need to explain anything. Your tears tell me that you are a safe person. So chill. I want to have this conversation with Emelda."

I stopped, and Emelda continued. Soon, this young lady prayed a dangerous prayer—asking God to forgive her of her sins and take over her life. As if on cue, the other team members showed up, and after exchanging phone numbers with her, we left her the contact information of the church and left.

By now the group was looking at me funny. I was smiling and crying at the same time. One of our team quipped, "If you go witnessing with Esteban today, you better take an umbrella! Because you're going to get wet!" I managed to laugh through the tears.

We ate lunch and then had a visit in the afternoon with a 70-year-old woman. After making introductions, I sat down on the couch next to the woman. She said, "I'm sad because my mother died this year." And she started to cry. What do you suppose I did? Yep, you guessed it. I joined right in! We cried a good cry together. And soon that woman turned her life over to the Lord. It was amazing. Walking away from that visit, I thought, "I don't understand what's happening here, but this has got to be the strangest and most exhilarating day I've ever lived."

But the day wasn't done. We had one more visit left that evening. We visited with the maid of one of the church members. At her house, her husband and two daughters, ages 14 and 11, were also present. We hit it off right away, and everyone was very happy. We all laughed together as they all seemed to be in such a good mood. Soon all four of them were responding to the invitation to place their faith in Christ. After their prayers, I thought, "This is great! These people became believers, and I didn't even have to cry!"

Then the maid looked at me and said, "You want to know why it was so easy for us to become believers tonight?"

"Please tell me," I replied.

"The first day that I walked into the home of my employers, there was a peace that I felt that I couldn't explain. And I wanted to know what it was. So, for the past six months, the lady of the house has been explaining what their faith is all about. When I'd learn something,

I'd come home and tell my kids and my husband. By tonight, we knew we wanted to pray to receive Christ. It was easy."

And then she asked, "Would you do something for me?"

"What's that?" I said.

"Would you pray a prayer of blessing over our home?" she requested. And pointing to her employer, who was seated on the other side of the room, she continued, "Would you pray that our home would have the same peace that their home has, so that whenever anyone walks into our door, they'll feel the same peace and joy I felt that day I walked into their house?"

"I'd love to," I responded.

So we stood in a circle and held hands. And I prayed. And yes, I cried again! In fact, we all did. We shared tears of joy for what God was doing in that home.

That night, when I went to bed, I was in awe. Never in my life had I experienced a day like that. Never had I spent a day witnessing in which every single person who needed to make a decision for Christ did. And it hit me. I remembered my dangerous prayer—"Lord, make me your witness." I realized that I was right in the middle of seeing God answer that dangerous prayer.

As I stared at the ceiling, I asked the Father, "What happened today? What was the difference?" As I meditated on that question, I realized something for the first time—I have a ministry of tears.

So often, we think we have to witness and minister with strength, with airtight reasons, and with logic—when most times, God wants us to simply go in our weaknesses, in our frailties, and in our tears. The Apostle Paul put it this way, "When I am weak, He is made strong."

I believe that Paul could speak powerfully from personal experience, that the greater the pain in your life, the greater the potential for you to encourage someone else going through a similar ordeal. The weak encourage better than the strong, as odd as that sounds, but think about it. Who is likely to be the best encourager of a cancer patient, someone who's dealt with and battled cancer, or someone who has had perfect health his or her entire life? No question, right? Who's going to help someone heal after a loved one committed suicide? You know full well—someone who has been there too and been carried by God through the emotional darkness of that same experience.

We could list hundreds of situations, but here's the point. The greater the depths of your pain, the greater your potential for encouraging others—even if you are not delivered or healed or fixed yet.

Some of the greatest encouragers I know have chronic situations that they are walking through each day with a sweetness of spirit, a purity of heart, and a great attitude that notices the good in their lives and others.

We serve a God who can take every one of our hurts and use them to help someone else. How will that ever happen in you? Only when you give your tears to God and are unashamed in shedding a tear or two with others.

Reflecting on that day in Costa Rica, I started thinking about the woman who lost her 32-year-old son, and it dawned on me. God loved that woman so much, that He sent a Gringo who lived several thousand miles away to come and cry with her for about five minutes. And then another thought hit me. God loved *me* so much, that he sent me several thousand miles away, so that I could go cry with her, so that I could be healed too.

I didn't realize the full extent of what got fixed in my soul until I got home from Costa Rica.

# Chapter Eight: I Think it's About...Forgiveness

*"Lord, how many times shall I forgive my brother when he sins against me? Up to seven times?" Jesus answered, "I tell you, not seven times, but seventy seven times."* Matthew 18:21-22

*"The kingdom of heaven is like a king who wanted to settle accounts with his servants. As he began the settlement, a man who owed him ten thousand talents (several million dollars) was brought to him. Since he was not able to pay, the master ordered that he and his wife and his children and all that he had be sold to repay the debt. The servant fell on his knees before him. 'Be patient with me,' he begged, 'and I will pay back everything.' The servant's master took pity on him, canceled the debt and let him go.*

*But when that servant went out, he found one of his fellow servants who owed him a hundred denarii (a few dollars). He grabbed him and began to choke him. 'Pay back what you owe me!' he demanded. His fellow servant fell to his knees and begged him, 'Be patient with me, and I will pay you back.' But he refused. Instead, he went off and had the man thrown into prison until he could pay the debt.*

*When the other servants saw what had happened, they were greatly distressed and went and told their master everything that had happened. Then the master called the servant in. 'You wicked servant,' he said, 'I canceled all that debt of yours because you begged me to. Shouldn't you have had mercy on your fellow servant just as I had on you?' In anger his master turned him over to the jailers to be tortured until he should pay back all he owed.*

*This is how my heavenly Father will treat each of you unless you forgive your brother from your heart."*

— Jesus' story from Matthew 18:23-35

When I got home, I checked my email. My co-pastor friend had sent me one. I clicked on it, and the message said, "Steve, I know you're probably in Costa Rica, but when you get back, I'd like to meet with you if you are willing to do so."

I shot back an email, "Sure! Tell me when and where."

He replied, "How about tomorrow, in the park behind your house, at 3 p.m.?"

I typed, "Great! See you there," and clicked send.

Then I started to think more about what was happening. He wanted to meet me—in the park—behind my house—on my turf—on my holy ground! He knew what the park was for me. So I figured, "He's on my turf, and I'm gonna be ready for this!"

Well, the next day, at 3 p.m., I walked out the back of our house to go look for him. I was both apprehensive and pumped all at the same time. After seeing him on the other side of the park, I high stepped through some tall grass toward him. Without thinking, once I got up to him, I gave him a big bear hug and said, "How's it going bro'?"

"I'm doing okay, but it looks like you're doing great," he said.

I don't know what tipped him off, but he was right. I was doing great. I couldn't help but talk about my trip. And at one point, I looked at him, calling him by name, and said, "You know what? This experience in Costa Rica was so rich and meaningful, that if I had to go through the last 6 months again just so I'd have the Costa Rica experience, I'd do it all again."

Visibly moved, he said, "Wow."

We talked about an hour or so more, and toward the end, he said, "Steve, it's obvious that you are further along than I am. I hope and pray that one day I can get where you are."

As I hiked back home, I realized that the miracle of forgiveness was now complete in me. Before my trip, I had been working hard at forgiving him. Hey, I'm a pastor. I know all the stuff about how refusing to forgive can lead to bitterness and that bitterness is a cancer that eats at your soul. But the truth was, for many months I worked at forgiveness. I had to psych myself up to forgive. But now, it seemed I didn't have to work at it anymore. All I had left for my friend was love. In fact, I got to thinking, "Who could I blame for my trip to Costa Rica?" It was him! If he hadn't done what he did, I'd have never experienced the miracles I'd experienced. And at that point, it didn't matter who was wrong or right. That was all in the hands of God, and He had done a masterful job of turning it all around for my good.

That experience propelled me to a new awareness of how God is not limited by our circumstances. In Costa Rica our team saw more than 125 people come to Christ. And because of the deep friendships forged with others on that trip, I received invitations to go to Guatemala and Panama. The net result was that in a year when I had no official ministry, I saw more than 500 people come to Christ! And as of this writing, I'm still riding the waves of adventure that God began in that era of suffering and brokenness.

In addition, it led me on a quest to understand more about what this "suffering clause" is all about. During my walks I began to put some of the biblical pieces together and search the scriptures for how suffering fits into the life of a Christian. Is it really for all believers? Is it consistent with other teachings in the Bible? And most importantly, did Jesus have something to say about all this?

For me, the answers came when I began with Jesus. Did He promise his followers a life of suffering? And what exactly did He promise? I found four things that Jesus promised His followers.

You might want to pull out a note pad. I've got a diagram I want to show you, and you might want to draw it for yourself. But do me a favor. Promise me you won't laugh at my artwork!

PART TWO

# Jesus
# and the
# Suffering Clause

# Chapter Nine: Jesus' Promises to His Followers

*Then Peter began to mention all that he and the other disciples had left behind. "We've given up everything to follow you," he said. And Jesus replied, "I assure you that everyone who has given up house or brothers or sisters or mother or father or children or property, for my sake and for the Good News, will receive now in return, a hundred times over, houses, brothers, sisters, mothers, children, and property—with persecutions. And in the world to come they will have eternal life."*

Mark 10:28-30 (New Living Translation)

What did Jesus promise His followers? That was the question I asked myself as I reread the four gospels in one day, looking specifically for this answer. It wasn't long until I saw a couple of promises on two ends of the spectrum.

On one end, I saw that Jesus promised His followers great joy. In fact, He said that He came that our joy would be full and that it would be complete.

> *"I have told you this so that my joy may be in you and that your joy may be complete." John 15:11*

He promised other joyful byproducts of peace and ministry effectiveness—even saying that some would do greater things than He did, which is a staggering thought. But at the very least, He is referring to a joy dimension. It is at one end of the spectrum...

On the other end of the continuum is what? It's suffering. Jesus said,

*"In this world, you will have trouble." John 16:33*

He didn't say "might;" He said "will." Jesus also called each of us to take up our cross and follow Him—not exactly an invitation to a picnic in the park. This promise of suffering was not a hidden thought for Jesus. He said this in dozens of different ways and in many different teaching situations. I'll elaborate more on that in a minute.

So now, our picture looks like this...

Joy ———————— Suffering

But that's not all Jesus promised. He promised that those who followed Him and received the gift of salvation would wind up in heaven when they died. John 3:16 tells us that.

*God so loved the world, that he gave his one and only Son, that whoever believes in him shall not perish but have eternal life. John 3:16*

So now our picture has a heaven dimension to it.

But this isn't all. There's one more big promise Jesus made to us, and it ties everything together. It's the clenching promise in the Great Commission.

*"Surely I will be with you always, to the very end of the age." Matthew 28:20*

This is Jesus' amazing promise of His presence. And through the Holy Spirit, Jesus is with us. So now our diagram looks like this...

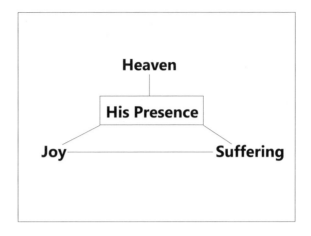

Having Jesus' presence with us transforms everything. And it separates what we have as Christians with what non-Christians don't have.

Let's go back to the chart depicting joy and suffering. When we look at people who are not following Christ, there is a measure of joy and suffering in most of their lives, right? People can have enjoyable experiences. And they will suffer as they go through life, too. So what is the difference between our lives and theirs? It is the promise of His presence.

When Jesus, through the Holy Spirit, is present with us, He transforms our joy into something that is indescribable. Our joys become more than just fun fixes with temporary highs. They go deep into the soul.

And when He is present with us in our suffering, even that difficult state becomes something that can produce a deep kind of contentment that the scriptures describe as the "peace that passes all understanding." I've experienced it, and it's what James called a "pure" joy. I'll come back to that in a minute.

Additionally, when we go to heaven, it is Jesus' presence that is part of what makes heaven so good.

So when we boil it all down, the presence of Jesus is the centerpiece. His presence is what tilts joy into a deeper and richer kind of joy. His presence is what turns suffering from being a pure liability into something that is invaluable and life-enriching. And His presence is what is at the heart of what heaven is all about.

Because of Jesus' presence, the life He calls us to is one with a no-lose proposition—not because we won't face troubles, but because our troubles don't have the last word on our lives. His presence in our lives changes everything.

To give you more perspective on the suffering Jesus promised, I want to go back and give you some context to the passage in Mark 10 that we read at the beginning of the chapter.

Jesus had an interesting exchange with a rich, young yuppie. This guy wanted to know what it would take for him to go to heaven, and Jesus told him to sell everything he had, give his money to the poor, and come follow Him. The man's face fell and he left sad, because he couldn't do it. Bewildered, the disciples looked at Jesus and said, "If he can't make it? Who can?"

"With man it's impossible, but with God all things are possible," Jesus said.

Then Peter, still thinking about how the silver-spooned young man couldn't divest of his stuff, began to brag a bit about him and his buddies.

> Then Peter began to mention all that he and the other disciples had left behind. "We've given up everything to follow you," he said. And Jesus replied, "I assure you that everyone who has given up house or brothers or sisters or mother or father or children or property, for my sake and for the Good News, will receive now in return, a hundred times over, houses, brothers, sisters, mothers, children, and property—with persecutions. And in the world to come they will have eternal life."
>
> Mark 10:28-30 (New Living Translation)

Did you catch what Jesus said? He said that in this life we have the opportunity to experience a one-hundred-fold benefit now and eternal life when we die. But in listing the benefits, he mentions what? Persecutions! Persecutions? Yep. Persecutions. And the way he listed it, persecutions was not listed as a liability, but as a part of the hundred-fold benefit! This so intrigued me that I pulled out the Greek and looked to see if this was translated right.

What do you think I found? Well, when I looked at it, persecution really was tied to the sentence structure listing the benefits. It was thrown into the plus side of the equation. As I pondered various ways to see this connection, I remembered the Beatitudes of Jesus in his famous sermon on the mount. In Matthew 5:10, he said,

> *"Blessed are those who are persecuted because of righteousness..."*
> *Matthew 5:10*

In Phillip Yancey's book, *The Jesus I Never Knew*, he mentioned that some scholars have said that a good translation for the idea of "blessed" is "lucky" or "fortunate."[1]

I remembered that and how the word "lucky" unlocked an intriguing dimension to the Beatitudes for me. I began to consider the persecution angle and mentally began to replace "blessed" with "lucky" in that previous verse. So I reread it.

> *"Lucky" are those who are persecuted for righteousness.*

Lord, did you say "lucky?" Surely not. But I continued to look at the passage as Jesus goes on...

> *"Blessed (lucky) are you when people insult you, persecute you and falsely say all kinds of evil against you because of me. Rejoice and be glad, because great is your reward in heaven..." Matthew 5:11-12*

If I needed more evidence, I got it. Jesus made it abundantly clear that we can rejoice in persecutions because of what God does about it in heaven. There's a reward factored into heaven. But we don't have to wait until heaven for the benefit. We could start with the rejoicing now! Amazing!

When Jesus taught this concept and really honed in on rejoicing in persecution, people didn't know what to do with it. Even for His disciples, they had a hard time reconciling suffering with joy.

After Jesus' resurrection from the dead, He appeared to a couple of followers who felt disoriented after the crucifixion and the first reports of an empty tomb. They didn't recognize Jesus, so Jesus walked with them for a good ways on the road. These followers couldn't figure out why Jesus had to suffer and die. And Jesus, disguised as a fellow traveler, walked with them and taught them for several miles about how this was all part of God's plan. He said...

> *"Did not the Christ have to suffer these things and then enter his glory?" And beginning with Moses and all the Prophets, he explained to them what was said in all the Scriptures concerning himself.* Luke 24:26

You wonder if He mentioned Isaiah 53, the "suffering servant" passage that says,

> *He was despised and rejected by men, a man of sorrows, and familiar with suffering...Isaiah 53:3*

Or a few lines down in verse 10...

> *It was the Lord's will to crush him and cause him to suffer...After the suffering of his soul, he will see the light of life and be satisfied; by his knowledge my righteous servant will justify many, and he will bear their iniquities.*
> *Isaiah 53:10, 11*

We don't know everything Jesus told those travelers, but we are told that Jesus made it plain from the scriptures that the suffering of the Messiah was part of God's plan.

As they approached their destination, Jesus acted like He wanted to go on a little further, but the two travelers insisted that He stay for a meal together. As Jesus broke bread, their eyes were opened to who their guest was, and, in an instant, Jesus disappeared.

After that, these two followers hurried back to headquarters in Jerusalem to report this appearance of Jesus and to share what He said about His suffering. As they were talking, Jesus appeared to the whole group and repeated much of the same things—emphasizing that He had to suffer before rising from the dead. It was a day none of them would forget.

And this is the marching band point I promised you several chapters ago. This is the ultimate, groundbreaking truth that can transform us in tough times. Here, Jesus gives us a solid foundation for dealing with suffering and forever ties our "suffering clause" concept to the "nail it" mentality I've advocated. Because of the very real presence of Jesus in our lives, joy, suffering, and heaven are all tied together into one life- transforming package. And the more we think about it in this way, the more we focus on what will help us thrive in whatever state of circumstances we find ourselves.

When we look at suffering the way Jesus did, we find ourselves in the ultimate no-lose position. Now we can run out onto the playing fields of life with a "go out and nail it" mentality focused on being faithful to His call on our lives. Our heavenly coach wants us in the game executing His play in His way. If we experience joy, great! If we suffer, fine. Suffering doesn't have the last word. And if we die, we gain—being in the presence of Jesus in heaven.

No doubt, Jesus made it known to His followers that suffering was a part of His plan and He wanted us to be ready for it. He didn't want any disciple of His to miss this crucial reality. And that leads me to the biggest question of the whole book.

What exactly is the secret to being able to outlast our tough times? How can we ensure that we're in that no-lose position where suffering doesn't sting us so hard? Let's tackle that question next.

# Chapter Ten: The Secret to Outlasting Tough Times...

*"Surely I will be with you always, to the very end of the age."*
—Jesus, Matthew 28:20

May I have the envelope? Drum roll please. The secret to outlasting tough times...is ...really not a secret at all! In fact, I gave it to you in the last chapter. What is it?

It is the presence of Jesus.

When we have and experience the presence of Jesus, we can outlast anything. That's the big secret.

When I wrote the first edition of the book, this chapter was not here. But after trying to coach some people who were stuck in their circumstances and who were having trouble experiencing the presence of Jesus, I realized that I overestimated our abilities to connect with Jesus. Truth be told, there were some things I was missing in my own understanding of all this. Thankfully, some of my friends helped me see this more clearly.

I think a big part of this is an undercurrent in our American culture that is so pervasive and so ingrained in our identity that we become blind to what other Christians in other parts of the world see so easily. In one word, our problem is "individualism." We so value individual freedom and our personal pursuit of happiness that we easily miss the communal ramifications of Jesus' teachings. Because of our obsession with the individual, when it comes to faith, we tend to preach a "just me and Jesus" brand of Christianity. Think about it. What are you told to do when you want to have a daily experience with Jesus?

When I ask this question in a group setting, I get two answers pretty quickly.

1.  I experience Jesus through prayer.
2.  I experience Jesus through reading the Bible.

In our American mindset, we think of doing lots of personal prayer and Bible study. So we read devotions. We buy journals, and we fill them with our thoughts. We fill in the blanks to discipleship notebooks. We memorize scriptures. We say our prayers. And oh, yes, on Sunday we go to a church building to sit in pews and listen to a preacher tell us what else we should do on our own when we go home. Almost everything we do is alone.

Now, please note that there is nothing wrong with these two things. I'm not against personal prayer and Bible study. You've already seen how I experienced Jesus' presence in my walks and in times of solitude. His presence in those dark days I told you about were so real and strong and so good that even to this day I sometimes want to go back to those places just to experience God in that way again.

But there is more to experiencing God than doing everything alone. When I ask groups to come up with another answer besides these first two, a lot of times the room gets quiet. Sometimes I have to keep prodding. But eventually someone says it in one way or another.

3. I experience Jesus through His body, the church!

I need to experience Jesus with skin on. When we are together, we embody the presence of Jesus to one another. Jesus said, "Where two or three are gathered in my name, I am in the midst of them." Paul said that when we get together, we are all different members of Jesus' body and have different functions.

We need to experience Jesus through each other. We need to experience the realities of Jesus in the church. And let me be frank. Sitting in rows listening to a preacher talk is not "church" in the biblical sense. "Church" is a collection of Jesus followers who are embodying the presence of Jesus through their mutual involvement in the lives of one another. No single person has a corner on Jesus. No isolated Christian has all the gifts. No solitary person can ever see a full picture of what God is up to in the world without being in touch with His body, the collection of followers that we call the church.

In this sense, small group Bible studies and house churches have a greater potential to give us a place to experience the presence of Jesus than can large group services that have a preacher and a small group of musicians doing all the work for us. In the New Testament, there are a lot of "one another" teachings to the church, indicating our need to be connected to one another to be able to give and receive and embody Jesus' presence to each other. I am convinced that much of our trouble in feeling connected with God is because we have isolated ourselves from God's presence in our brothers and sisters in Christ.

I'll be honest. There are times when in my personal walk with Jesus, I don't feel His presence as acutely as maybe at other times. I have learned that it is precisely at those times that I need to have a loving community of Christ followers who will love me and carry me and be present with me so that I can experience this third dimension of having Jesus present with me when times are tough.

And because I can readily see that I need this, I need to make myself available to others so that they can experience this reality as well. I think this is what the New Testament writer of Hebrews was referring to when he said:

> Let us not give up meeting together as some are in the habit of doing, but let us encourage one another... Hebrews 10:25

In order that we experience Jesus in community, we have to be devoted not only to Jesus, but to one another—to the "fellowship" as it is mentioned in Acts chapter 2.

I offer further thoughts related to this in coming chapters, so I will resist the temptation to dump a truckload of information on you here. But let me say this to make sure we're tracking with one another about the secret to outlasting tough times.

Your participation in a loving Jesus community of brothers and sisters is crucial to you experiencing Jesus during tough times. Don't drop this ball! Stay connected. Do not allow yourself to get isolated from the body of Christ. You may not see the need for this now, but believe me there will come a day when you will be desperate for someone with skin on to reflect the presence of Jesus to you. Prepare today for that reality.

Speaking of Jesus with skin on, I want to ask a historical question with regard to the earliest disciples being equipped to be there for each other during tough times. Can we see from historical records whether or not the early disciples "got it" and handled suffering and persecution well? After Jesus' resurrection, did they live out the rest of their lives with confidence and courage and a "nail it" attitude no matter what the cost and no matter what the circumstances?

I can hardly wait to share with you what I found. Let's look at that in the next chapter.

# Chapter Eleven: In His Steps...

*"It is commendable if a man bears up under the pain of unjust suffering because he is conscious of God. But how is it to your credit if you receive a beating for doing wrong and endure it? But if you suffer for doing good and you endure it, this is commendable before God. To this you were called, because Christ suffered for you, leaving you an example, that you should follow in his steps."*

—Peter, 1 Peter 2:19-21

Before I answer the question of the previous chapter, I think it would be good to state the obvious from Peter's words to us that we have just read.

First, to follow Jesus' teaching about suffering, we don't need to go out picking a fight—looking for trouble. Troubles and persecutions will find us. We do not need to be gluttons for punishment.

Second, suffering that we endure for doing what is right and good is the commendable kind, and that's what this book is primarily about. Here, I don't want to talk a lot about the suffering that we deserve because of our own stupidity or humanity, because I will deal with that in later chapters.

But for now, it's good to ask, "Did I do this to myself?" In my own life, I'd say that maybe 80% of my suffering is my own fault. I'm not proud of that, but it's true for me. When that's the case, I need to humbly go to God or others and ask for forgiveness and beg God to have mercy on me and help me. Admitting my own sin and stupidity is not particularly noble; it's just a matter of dealing with life responsibly.

However, sometimes, things just happen. Calamity strikes in a way that I can't control. Someone hurts me or misunderstands me or chooses to harm me. Sometimes I even suffer for being a follower of Christ or for trying to do my best in leading people in the church.

When suffering fits in this category, then we're ready to talk about the question in the previous chapter. Let me repeat the question.

When did the disciples "get it" and begin to understand some of what Jesus told them about suffering?

Only after they went through the suffering themselves and remembered what Jesus said could they put it all together and really understand what Jesus taught them. Before it was a reality, it was an impossible-to-understand theory.

And in the words of Peter, it was only in the experiences of "walking in His steps" that they got it. Let me repeat that verse...

*"But if you suffer for doing good and you endure it, this is commendable before God. To this you were called, because Christ suffered for you, leaving you an example, **that you should follow in his steps**." 1 Peter 2:20-21*

Since Peter wrote these words, let's take his development as a case study here.

In Mark 8, Peter yo-yos from being a great positive example to being a great negative example for other followers of Jesus. In this chapter, when Jesus asked, "Who do you say that I am?"

Peter said, "You are the Christ." That confession was a big deal, and Peter must have been pleased with his statement of faith.

But immediately following that, Jesus began to teach the disciples that He would have to suffer many things and be rejected by the religious leaders. Peter spoke up again to rebuke Jesus and tell him that this should not be the plan. Remember what Jesus told Peter? He said, "Get behind me, Satan! You are speaking now for the devil himself."

Clearly, at this point, Peter didn't *get* this suffering thing. He flunked in the worst way. But let's not be too hard on him. We don't see that any of the others *got it* either. Even at the last supper, they still didn't understand Jesus' words about suffering. And, their "who's the greatest" argument prompted Jesus' foot-washing lesson—indicating the disciples were slow in adopting Jesus' servant leadership style, too.

After Jesus predicted Peter's denials, Peter swore he'd stay true, but he didn't. After Jesus' resurrection, Jesus had to reinstate a broken Peter to his leadership role in feeding and loving the brothers.

It was only after the resurrection, and after Peter and the rest of the disciples began to endure persecution, that they began to write as Peter did in 1 Peter. He tells new believers to rejoice in their salvation, and then says...

> *In this you greatly rejoice, though now for a little while you may have had to suffer grief in all kinds of trials. These have come so that your faith—of greater worth than gold, which perishes even though refined by fire—may be proved genuine and may result in praise, glory and honor when Jesus Christ is revealed. 1 Peter 1:6-7*

How could Peter say this now? I believe it was because he had been to the depths of despair and lived through it. He had walked in Jesus' steps. He'd been to prison. He'd been beaten. He'd been misunderstood. And he had experienced the real-life grace and forgiveness and the blessing of the presence of Jesus Himself in the middle of his own suffering.

The other disciples felt the same way. And James, Jesus' brother who didn't believe in Jesus during His ministry on earth, but who believed after seeing Him following the resurrection, wrote this.

> *Count it pure joy, my brothers, whenever you face trials of many kinds, because you know that the testing of your faith develops perseverance. Perseverance must finish its work so that you may be mature and complete, not lacking anything. James 1:2-3*

James nailed it. Using the joy/suffering continuum, James advises us to move suffering over to the joy category—but not just joy, but "pure" joy. Why? Because your suffering is going to give you a track toward perseverance and a maturity and something that actually completes you as a person.

Working backwards from this verse, we could ask the question, "Do you want to be mature and complete—having it all?" All of us would probably answer "yes." Then you'll need the quality of perseverance. Maturity won't come in a day. You ask, "How can we get a persevering spirit?" You're going to need some trials to test your faith.

This cracks me up. We go to God wanting the ability to handle any problem that comes our way. How do we get it? We have to have patience. How do we get patience? We have to have problems! It's inevitable! We can't bypass the spiritual weight room. If we want strong muscles, we need to press against the resistance to get strong.

So, when you get those opportunities to persevere, keep the end result in mind. The test you face is what will form you into a person who has everything. Look for the joy in that end result—even when it's hard.

Let's look at the disciples after Jesus' resurrection. In Acts, Dr. Luke tells us that the believers rejoiced at their opportunity to suffer for the cause of Christ. They not only believed what Jesus said about this, they lived it and experienced the reality of suffering for their Lord. And, if church history is accurate, they died being faithful in the middle of great affliction. Nearly every disciple eventually died a martyr's death for his steadfast belief in Jesus. According to church history, only John is said to have not been martyred like the other disciples. Early church historians report that he lived to a ripe old age of 100 and died of old age. Still, these accounts speak of him effectively dealing with being exiled to the isle of Patmos and suffering for the cause of Christ. He took a strong stand for Jesus in the face of Domitian, a Roman Emperor who had thousands of Christians executed. And John risked his life on many occasions to share the good news of Jesus.

So, did the disciples *get it* in regard to understanding Jesus' call to suffer? No doubt, they *got it*. And this characteristic spread to the other Christian leaders who followed them. James, Jesus' brother, got it and died a martyr's death, as did Paul, who reportedly was beheaded. And following them were many other leaders who lived well, suffered well, and died well.

But that leads to another question. With all this talk about the leaders of the church, is this kind of suffering primarily for pastor types and church leaders, or is there a suffering clause built into the life and calling of every believer?

Let's tackle that next.

PART THREE

# Further Implications of the Suffering Clause

# Chapter Twelve: Who Gets to Suffer...

*"If anyone would come after me, he must deny himself and take up his cross daily and follow me. For whoever wants to save his life will lose it, but whoever loses his life for me will save it. What good is it for a man to gain the whole world, and yet lose or forfeit his very self?"*

— Jesus, Luke 9:23-25

*"...everyone who wants to live a godly life in Christ Jesus will be persecuted..."*

— Paul, 2 Timothy 3:12

I think that by now you know the answer to the question, "Who gets to suffer?" It's anyone who chooses to follow Jesus. Suffering has no "non-clergy" exemption. All who follow Christ "get to" suffer. "Taking up our cross" is something that we are all called to do as we come to Jesus and follow Him. Every follower in every part of the world needs to be prepared to suffer. But rather than resigning ourselves to a joyless journey through tough times, we need to see it like those in the early church saw it—suffering is both a privilege and a responsibility to those who follow Christ.

In the book of Acts, Peter and the other leaders had been greatly slandered and maligned by the religious leaders in Jerusalem. After some jail time and some rough questioning by the Sanhedrin, they returned to the other believers and did what? Did they gather signatures for a petition? Did they pout and cry because of the opposition? No. They got back together and rejoiced that God saw them worthy to suffer for the cause of Christ. (Acts 5:41)

When I compare this attitude with our Christian culture in the U.S. today, it can be striking. I can't remember the last time I heard anyone from my part of the Midwest come to a prayer meeting and say, "Hey everybody, gather around. I just got blasted for my faith today.

Break out the chips and salsa! Let's party!" But that seems to be closer to the heart of the early church. Are we missing something in our safe, North American version of Christianity?

I think we can learn from Christians in other places. In the early 70's, when I was about 12 years old, my family lived in Peru. During part of our time there, major political unrest plagued the country. At one point, the police and the military were fighting, leaving the nation paralyzed. The military dictator put a curfew in place, and any group of more than five people was deemed illegal. We had five in our family, so if we got together with anyone else, we'd be violating the law.

The first Sunday after the new martial law was in place, our family got ready for church as we had always done. I asked my father, "Dad, if we go to church and other people show up today, will we be illegal?"

"Yes."

"Do you think anyone else will be there?"

"Son, I don't know."

As we rode to church, the streets were eerily empty. When we arrived and entered the building, we noticed that our family and a handful of other people were all who had made it there. Latin Americans are known to show up to meetings late, but even for them, this was unusual. But a few more came in, and the adults decided to start the service. As we started to sing, people started to trickle in by two's and three's. Soon we had a decent crowd, and the singing got louder with the additional voices. After one song, we sang another and then another. After about an hour, the church was packed like I'd never seen it before. And those singing were singing with tears in their eyes. No one knew if this might be the last time that we could be together as a congregation. And by their presence, they were making an emphatic statement that they wanted to be counted with their brothers and sisters in Christ. To cap off that morning, the whole congregation sang Peru's national anthem. I can still hear them belt out the words in Spanish, "Somos libres seamos! Lo siempre seamos lo siempre!" Translated it means, "We're free, yes we're free! Always and forever!"

For these dear believers, that day their love of God, love of country, and love for each other in the church body was tested like never before. And they passed the test with a great resolve and a great demonstration of faith.

Looking back, that experience marked me in ways I couldn't have understood as a child. I think it gave me a lifelong desire to live for Christ as courageously as these people did. And it prompted me to pay attention to what happens when believers face persecution. Through the years, I've seen a consistent pattern. Persecution can never thwart the effects of true Christianity. In fact, persecution has a way of bringing out the best in Jesus' followers.

Curtis Sergeant, a missionary friend from Asia, told me several stories of the persecution that took place in a region where he worked with underground churches. The churches in this network began a process of multiplying spontaneously. In 1993, there were three house churches there. By 1998, there were 550 churches and over 55,000 converts.

Some might say that fast growth produces weaker growth, but that was not the case here. Curtis said that even the newest of believers often exhibited faith that would put many of us to shame. He gave us one example that I'll never forget.

A group of believers in one particular village were praying for a neighboring village. After praying, they sent several men to go to this village and share with them about their faith in Jesus. When they got to the edge of the town, some men stopped them and asked about their intentions. One of the men said, "We're here to share with you about how Jesus has changed the lives of several of us in our village."

"Our village belongs to the spirits," one villager said. "We don't want to have anything to do with you." Then they pounced on them and began to kick and punch these Christians. One man was literally beaten to death. Those who survived retreated back to their village.

As that little congregation gathered around to pray, their prayers were desperate and heartfelt. After several days of prayer, they began to sense that God wanted them to go back, so they asked, "Who among us feels called to go back?"

One woman raised her hand. "I do," she said. It was the widow of the man who was killed.

"But what if something happens to you?" others protested. "Your kids will be orphans."

"God wants me to go," the widow said.

So, she went back with the other two men who survived.

As they approached the village, the same men came up to stop them. "Let me go in front," the widow said to the other two. Before they could hold her back, she stepped forward and said to the approaching group, "I am the widow of the man you killed. And I want you to know that if my husband were alive, he would want to tell you that he forgives you. And as I come to you today, I want you to know that I forgive you. The only way I can do this is because of what Jesus has done for me. If you want to know more about this, then tell others in the village that we will meet with you under that tree in an hour."

Instead of a violent response, they listened and then went back into their village. Soon, many people gathered. And in a short time, many had come to Christ. This woman had been a believer for five months, yet she exhibited a maturity and a love that far surpassed her new believer status.

I asked Curtis about this response to persecution that he saw. He said that these people see persecution as a blessing. If they get thrown in jail, they say, "Great! Now I can evangelize the jail." If they then get thrown into solitary confinement, they say, "Wonderful! Now I can focus on prayer and getting close to God." If the authorities take their house, they say, "That's okay. Now I can focus on my heavenly home." If they face being killed for their faith, they say, "That means I get to go to heaven and be with my Lord." This irrepressible spirit matches up to the words of Paul, who wrote toward the end of his ministry...

*"For to me, to live is Christ, and to die is gain." Philippians 1:21*

If I live, I get to point people to Christ. If I die, I get to be with Him forever. I can't lose.

Those Asian Christians had mastered Paul's approach to life. If they faced troubles here, God could use them to bring glory to Himself and draw other people into a loving relationship with Him too. If they died, they got heaven. What more could they want?

How does that compare to your experience? Most of us in North America marvel at that kind of faith but can hardly imagine ourselves in that situation. Yet, the suffering clause remains for us. How does it work here in the U.S.? Truthfully, I think we've been sold a bill of goods, and you may not like what I'm about to say.

# Chapter Thirteen: A Bill of Goods...

*I pray that you may prosper in all things and be in health, just as your soul prospers.* 3 John 1:2 (NKJV)

*He himself bore our sins in His body on the tree, so that we might die to sins and live for righteousness; by his wounds you have been healed.* 1 Peter 2:24

*To keep me from becoming conceited because of these surpassingly great revelations, there was given me a thorn in my flesh, a messenger of Satan, to torment me. Three times I pleaded with the Lord to take it away from me. But he said to me, "My grace is sufficient for you, for my power is made perfect in weakness." Therefore I will boast all the more gladly about my weaknesses, so that Christ's power may rest on me. That is why, for Christ's sake, I delight in weaknesses, in insults, in hardships, in persecutions, in difficulties. For when I am weak, then I am strong.*

— Paul, 2 Corinthians 12:7-10

At the risk of stirring up a little controversy among Christians, I want to speak plainly about how I believe that we have been sold a theological bill of goods in our country. Many Christians today adhere to what some would call a "health and wealth" gospel. It's a gospel or message that says that if I am in God's will, I will be healthy and wealthy. Some might even quote 3 John 1:2 that I listed above and say, "See, God wants us all to be healthy and prosper."

Let's look closer at this verse to see it from a couple of different angles. First, this was written by John, one of Jesus' closest followers and friends. By this point in his life and ministry, he was the elder statesmen for Christians living in the region of Ephesus, now modern day Turkey. During that time, Christians were under persecution in many places. Not long after John penned these words, he was taken by the Roman officials and put on his exile island—the island of Patmos. On that island John wrote the book of Revelation to encourage his flock to hang in there during tough times.

Secondly, John's note in this letter was written to a friend to take care of a problem in one of the house churches. Essentially, John started his letter with a line saying, "I hope you're doing well—that you're healthy and prosperous." Then he talked about the problem.

Let me ask you a question. Isn't it normal letter writing protocol to say something like, "I hope you're doing well" in a letter to a friend? Just because you say that to someone, does it mean that you believe that everyone everywhere is destined by God to be healthy and wealthy at all times? That just doesn't make sense when we look at the track record of the early church—dealing with all kinds of trials of life and death and being an underground movement in a hostile Roman empire.

Also, looking at the idea of prosperity here, note that John said that he hoped his friend prospered just like his soul prospered. I believe that this certainly implies that there is a lot of room for prospering in ways other than financially or materially. The early believers were well acquainted with a prosperity of the soul that transcends how good we feel or how deep our pockets are.

To answer the question, "Are Christians called to be healthy and wealthy?" the biblical answer is that some are and some aren't. Health and wealth is not the ultimate issue. Whether we are healthy and wealthy, or if we are sick and poor, the call is the same for every follower of Jesus. We are called to follow our Leader. In whatever state we are, we are called to serve God and other people.

With that said, we don't have to shy away from prayers for healing and seeking God's miraculous provision for us. The early followers did that and saw many miracles take place. In my own experience today, I have sought people to pray for me. In fact many have prayed for my health and the financial resources I needed. In all of this, I am convinced that God has been 100% faithful to me.

To say that *all* dedicated followers of Christ should be healthy and wealthy is a dangerous position to take, because it can wreak havoc on the tender faith of sincere followers of Jesus who are new to their faith or who are going through a particularly tough time with no apparent rhyme or reason for it.

And speaking of Jesus, look at his experience. Jesus did not have material wealth during his days on the earth, and he certainly didn't go to the cross for his health. One of the popular health and wealth verses cited is the line at the beginning of this chapter that says of Jesus that it is "by his wounds" that we are healed. Some say that this indicates that because of Jesus' torture on the cross, we will now be healed in our bodies. But the context of that statement was clearly dealing with our woundedness as sinners in need of a Savior.

Similarly, Paul, arguably one of the greatest Christians of all time, didn't live up to a "health and wealth" gospel. We know that on the health end he pleaded with God for a result he never got. Would you go to Paul and tell him that he didn't "name it and claim it" right? I know I wouldn't want to fly that one by the old Apostle. On the wealth side, he always had enough, but he talked about how he had learned to be content with little.

As a pastor and friend, I've walked alongside many who have gotten disillusioned over this issue. I've seen people step out in faith—trying to do the right thing, but something went wrong. Either their plan didn't work, or someone got hurt, or sick, or died. I've seen trouble when someone locked horns with someone else and conflict entered their reality. Many a wounded person has come to me and asked, "What did I do wrong?" Really, that question is more of a statement. If I were to reword their question to accurately describe their dilemma, it might be, "I know that when we step out in faith, if we do it right, everything is supposed to go well. If it doesn't go well, then I must be outside of God's will. So please tell me what I'm doing wrong."

Granted, we can be wrong in some way that we don't understand, but there is the possibility that God might call us to step out in faith and then go through a tough time that doesn't include ease and comfort. Sometimes God leads us to problems, difficulties, and disappointments. Sometimes God allows us to get whacked even when we're not outside of His will.

For many of us, because our suffering may not be a life and death proposition, we can lose the sense of what suffering is all about. I think for those of us in the United States, where most aren't persecuted like our brothers and sisters in other places in the world, suffering can be hard to understand. Still, we know it is a reality for so many people.

I believe we suffer because we don't know how to suffer. I believe that we suffer most in our country because of our unwillingness to embrace suffering. Many spend their lives in suffering avoidance. Some hope to wish away their troubles. Others harbor anger at God for dealing them such a wretched hand in life. Whether our suffering is considered big or small, the net result is the same. We can live life in a miserable, joyless state, and miss the best God has for us, or we can live in the no-lose state where we can enjoy good times and bad.

If most of us don't know how to suffer well, then a perceptive question is, "How do we 'learn' to suffer?" I think that answer comes by looking at Paul's options. When Paul didn't get what he wanted, he really only had a couple of basic options. One, he could bemoan the fact that God let him down and get bitter. Or, he could trust God to sort it all out in the end. Obviously, he chose the latter.

For us, it's no different. Whether our suffering is big or small, whether we think it counts in eternity or not, our choices are similar to Paul's. We can bemoan the suffering that comes our way, or we can become trophies of God's grace where we boast in what He's done in our weaknesses. Paul got to live long enough that he could boast in his weaknesses because of the way God used them for His glory.

Maybe you haven't lived that long yet. But take Paul's attitude to the bank and cash it. In God's economy, His power is made most evident in our weaknesses and not in our strengths. And the longer you trust Him in this, the more you will see that Paul was right.

With this thought in mind, are you in a position of trust before the Lord, or is something getting in the way? Are you longing to courageously live in a Paul-like trusting relationship with God but seem to be shrinking back in fear?

If fear grips you, then you'll want to experience the unconventional way the early church dealt with their fears. It's inspiring.

# Chapter Fourteen: Bold Love...

*"There is no fear in love. But perfect love drives out fear, because fear has to do with punishment. The man who fears is not made perfect in love."*
—the Apostle John, 1 John 4:18

*"Love knows no limit to its endurance, no end to its trust, no fading of its hope; it can outlast anything. Love still stands when all else has fallen."*
—the Apostle Paul, 1 Corinthians 13:7-8

Fear was real for those early followers of Jesus. But they had something bigger—something more powerful. It was love—a really bold love.

The Apostle Paul put it this way in a letter to some church friends in Corinth...

*Three things will last forever—faith, hope, and love—and the greatest of these is love.*
1 Corinthians 13:13 (New Living Translation)

One of the unfortunate realities about our English language is the imprecise way it describes "love." We can "love" our spouse, we can "love" a child, and we can "love" a friend. But we can also "love" pizza, and chocolate, and someone's hair, and even our dog! No offense to dog lovers out there, but there is a difference between the way I love my dog and the way I love my spouse!

Greek, the language Paul used to write his letters, is much more sophisticated and precise in its capability of describing the word "love." "Eros" is one Greek word for love that describes sensual and romantic love. "Storge" is a word that speaks of a natural, family kind of love between mothers and fathers and brothers and sisters. "Phileo" is a word that speaks of brotherly love, not just in the family sense, but in the sense of friendship and close connection to others in a loving community. And then finally, there is the word "agape." "Agape" is a sacrificial, unconditional love that runs supreme to all other loves.[1]

Granted, there is some overlay of these words in Greek usage where they can be interchangeable in certain contexts. But the interesting thing to note about those who followed Jesus and later wrote about it is that they used the word "agape" much more prevalently than the average person writing in Greek in that day.[2] "Agape" is the word that Paul chose when he waxed eloquently about love's supremacy. John, Jesus' close follower who we have mentioned several times already in this book, harped on agape love in both his eyewitness accounts about Jesus and in his letters written to encourage people to keep on loving their way through tough times and seemingly hopeless situations.

One such hopeless situation came when Jesus was crucified on the cross. After the crucifixion, it seemed that all was lost. Fear struck the hearts of all those who followed Jesus. To be sure, even after the resurrection, they were still afraid. Would the Roman soldiers come to get them? Would the Jewish leaders concoct some half-baked charges and turn vicious again—like they did with Jesus?

Before the Jewish holiday of Pentecost, we're told that these fearful followers numbered at about 120. They huddled in desperate prayer vigils behind closed doors. Even though Jesus' post-resurrection appearances excited them and gave them hope, fear seemed to be hovering over them still.

On the day of Pentecost, just 50 days after the resurrection, everything changed. Something happened in their prayer gathering that caused them to come out onto the streets and speak boldly about Jesus. Because people came to Jerusalem from all over the world, the city was full of people speaking different languages. But amazingly those from other places heard the message in their own native tongues. Peter grew even bolder after onlookers mocked, "I think they're drunk!"

Peter climbed the temple steps and shouted, "Listen to me! All of you! These people aren't drunk. It's only nine in the morning! The prophet Joel forecasted this many years ago."

The people stopped what they were doing and listened. "This all points to Jesus," Peter declared. "He was the long awaited messiah. And you killed him! But God, in His sovereignty and His power, has raised this same Jesus from the dead." The message was riveting and bold.

When he finished, the people were cut to the heart and called out to Peter, "What should we do then?" And Peter told them to repent and be baptized—to turn their lives over to Jesus, asking for the forgiveness of their sins. And in unprecedented fashion, 3000 people were saved and then baptized that day.

From this point on, Jesus' followers got bolder. And their prayers reflected this new boldness. After a couple of incidents when Peter and the disciples had been detained by the authorities for street preaching, here's how they prayed in their prayer meeting...

> *"Now, Lord, consider their threats and enable your servants to speak your word with great boldness. Stretch out your hand to heal and perform miraculous signs and wonders through the name of your holy servant Jesus." After they prayed, the place where they were meeting was shaken. And they were all filled with the Holy Spirit and spoke the word of God boldly. Acts 4:29-31*

What made the difference? I would propose that the over-riding factor in turning cowards into heroes had to do with one thing—His presence. They flourished when God empowered them through His Holy Spirit. Remember the charts in chapter nine of what Jesus promised us? In dealing with fear, it is His presence that transforms us. His presence is what makes all the difference.

But what is it about His presence that does it? What does His presence feel like? For me, His presence feels like...love. Yes. It's love. Let's look at a couple of lines before that passage from 1 John that you read at the beginning of the chapter.

> *God is love. Whoever lives in love lives in God, and God in him. 1 John 4:16*

His presence in our lives has a love component that's tied to the very nature of God. God is love. If we are in His presence, then we are in the presence of true love. Then, here's the clincher.

*There is no fear in love. But perfect love drives out fear...*
*1 John 4:18*

How do love and fear interact? Love pushes fear to the side. Does it completely do away with it? I don't think it does. But love does seem to give us the ability to be bold.

Let's talk about bold love. A compelling example could be seen in observing an ordinary mother. She can be afraid of spiders and snakes and go into hysterics over the sight of a cockroach, but put her in a situation where her child is in danger, and she becomes Wonder Woman. That mother would never run into a burning building unless what? Yep. I think you're getting it...unless her baby was in that building. Her love would push aside her fears while she courageously imperiled her own life to save her child.

For the disciples, I believe that, as a result of their desperate prayer times, God's Spirit gave them a love for those around them that pushed back the fear of what might happen to them and gave them a boldness to share in public. Why did they share so boldly on the day of Pentecost? I think that in their prayer time, when God's Spirit came upon them, they got a portion of God's love for other people, and nothing can stop that kind of love. It's got to get out. Persecution can't stop it. Language barriers can't stop it. And the fears of rejection get pushed way to the side, as bold love repels our cowardly natures.

Let's bring this into our world. For us, a bold love can help us push back the fears of sicknesses, setbacks, and calamities. Why? Let's make sure we understand this—it's because we know that God's presence makes all the difference—turning whatever we might face into something of ultimate good. Paul said something about that in Romans 8:28, didn't he?

*We know that in all things God works for the good of those who love him, who have been called according to his purpose. Romans 8:28*

Paul went on to say...

*I am convinced that neither death nor life, neither angels nor demons, neither the present nor the future, nor any powers, neither height nor depth, nor anything else in all creation, will be able to separate us from the love of God that is in Christ Jesus our Lord.* Romans 8:38-39

Bold love. It comes from God, and as it fills us up, it pushes our fears of suffering to the side. Yes, our fears will exist, but they don't have to paralyze us or have a permanent grip on us—not when love is on our side.

This is great news! But before we all sing the "Hallelujah Chorus," I want to back up a step or two and make sure we realize that even with bold love filling our hearts, suffering is far from easy. Even for Jesus, suffering was hard. Let's look at His greatest struggle with this in the next chapter.

# Chapter Fifteen: Joy Revisited...

*Weeping may last for a night, but joy comes in the morning.*

Psalm 30:5

*They went to a place called Gethsemane, and Jesus said to his disciples, "Sit here while I pray." He took Peter, James and John along with him, and he began to be deeply distressed and troubled. "My soul is overwhelmed with sorrow to the point of death," he said to them. "Stay here and keep watch."*

*Going a little farther, he fell to the ground and prayed that if possible the hour might pass from him. "Abba, Father," he said, "everything is possible for you. Take this cup from me. Yet not what I will, but what you will."*

*Then he returned to his disciples and found them sleeping. "Simon," he said to Peter, "Are you asleep? Could you not keep watch for one hour? Watch and pray so that you will not fall into temptation. The spirit is willing, but the body is weak."*

*Once more he went away and prayed the same thing. When he came back, he again found them sleeping, because their eyes were heavy. They did not know what to say to him.*

*Returning the third time, he said to them, "Are you still sleeping and resting? Enough! The hour has come. Look, the Son of Man is betrayed into the hands of sinners. Rise! Let us go! Here comes my betrayer!"*

Mark 14:32-42

Fear of suffering is real. To deny our fear of suffering is to deny a part of what makes us human. To deny our fear of suffering is to deny something that even Jesus experienced. And before you get too nervous here, let's not even worry about which nature Jesus was in—His human or divine nature during this ordeal. Let's just let Jesus be Jesus. I really appreciate Mel Gibson's portrayal of Jesus agonizing in the garden in the movie, *The Passion of the Christ,* because I believe it accurately depicts the intense emotion of fear, suffering, and resolve that Jesus went through in those painful hours.

According to the gospels, the night before the crucifixion, Jesus was afraid. He longed for his friends to support Him in prayer. And He dreaded the suffering that He would endure. Luke writes that it was so intense that Jesus sweated drops of blood. What kept him on course?

Before we answer this, let's look at the anguish of Jesus as it's recorded in scripture in a little more depth. The passage at the beginning of this chapter is an amazing one. For someone going through suffering, I believe that this could very well be "the other Lord's Prayer." It can serve as a model for us—every bit as useful as the model prayer that we think of most often. (You know, the prayer that starts "Our Father, who art in heaven...") Well, instead of that one, let's look at *this* prayer of Jesus and take it line by line.

First, Jesus didn't want to be alone on this occasion. This is different from His prayer times where He broke away from the pack in solitude. This time, He needed the community. He needed His brothers to hold Him up in prayer, so He wanted them to join Him in this prayer time.

Jesus didn't hold back when He prayed. "God, my heart is so ripped up with sorrow that I think I'll die," He said. Then He looks back, "Hey you guys, are you still there? You're looking droopy eyed." Then He goes a little further from the group, but still in earshot, and pleads, "Abba! Daddy, would you please take this cup from me? I can't take it. This one is too hard!" And after what must have been a long pause, Jesus comes back and says, "Nevertheless, not My will, but Yours be done."

Jesus told us in the model prayer to use the intimate term of "Abba" to address God. Now, it's like He's pleading, "Dad, will you please get me out of this!" But when God said no, Jesus accepted His lot and submitted to the Father.

Have you ever thought that this could be a model for your prayer life when you are in the middle of suffering? Apparently, it's okay to go to God and say, "Hey! Dad! Help! Take this pain away. Take this situation and fix it. Do a miracle. Get me out of this jam." That kind of praying is what Jesus did, and it's exhibited as well in the Psalms where people like David poured out their broken hearts before God. But the prayer doesn't stop there. After Jesus pleads with God, He humbly accepts God's will.

Christians can get stuck on both sides of this equation. Some get stuck by not allowing themselves to fully pour out their hearts before God and ask Him for deliverance. Others get stuck by not coming to a place of total trust and acceptance of God's will for them in the moment. To follow Jesus, both are recommended. We are to go to Him with the worst of it, and we're to come out with a childlike trust that leaves it all in the hands of our good God who will perhaps one day show us the meaning and purpose behind our trials and sufferings.

Before I move on, we do need to try to answer the question I asked earlier. What do you think motivated Jesus to stay on course and go the way of the cross? The scripture tells us what it was:

> *Let us fix our eyes on Jesus, the author and perfecter of our faith, who for the joy set before him endured the cross, scorning its shame, and sat down at the right hand of the throne of God. Consider him who endured such opposition from sinful men, so that you will not grow weary and lose heart. Hebrews 12:2-3*

What kept Jesus on course? It was the joy set before Him. Jesus had to look past the present and see a joy-filled future. And what was that joy He saw? I think Jesus saw it on several levels. In the eternal scheme of things, I believe that Jesus looked forward to returning to His rightful place in heaven, in the loving community of God the Father and the Holy Spirit.

In the more immediate sense, I believe Jesus could see the joy on the faces of His disciples after they see their resurrected Lord. Jesus could see Peter on the other side of the resurrection being reinstated to great ministry effectiveness. He could see the thousands of people in Jerusalem being baptized after Peter's Pentecost sermon. He could see the courage of His ragtag band of followers spreading the good news in the region.

But further down the road, Jesus could see the huge impact on generations to come as God's redemptive plan was completed. Jesus could see the joy of connecting men and women to God both in the present and in eternity. Jesus could see that every person from every tribe and every nation and every ethnic background would be given a joyful alternative if He stayed the course.

And on a personal level, this translates that joy to you and me. I wonder if Jesus didn't have snapshots of us in mind during this ordeal—seeing the joy that would be brought to our lives because of His bold, sacrificial love that manifested itself on a cross and is symbolized by an empty tomb.

Jesus focused on future joy. And we can follow His lead. We too can hang on during our suffering knowing that joy is set before us if we can muster the strength to lift our gaze to the future God holds for us.

This goes back to chapter one and two where we looked at the way we think. Looking to future joy is a "nail it" way to think, and that mindset helps us endure suffering.

Let's take this to the weight room. How do you endure difficult workouts and grueling training regimens? You do it by keeping the prize in mind, the future joy that can come to those who persevere. You push through the pain of lifting those weights or running those sprints for the feeling of victory in the game, or for the joy of performing well under difficult circumstances, or for the satisfaction that you are growing stronger.

For the past few years, I have taken numerous trips to Guatemala. As we partner with the churches and leaders in that country, we have developed wonderful relationships with many people all over the country. We've run medical clinics, sports clinics, Guatemalan rodeos, pastor conferences, motorcycle rallies, leadership training, and more. Our main focus has been to partner with Guatemalan believers who want to go to the more difficult places in their country to share the transforming message of Jesus to people who have not had much contact with that message. In many of our partnerships, we can see hundreds of people come to a decision to follow Jesus. It is truly amazing.

Several years ago, we went to a remote jungle area to show the *Jesus* movie in the Kekchi language. This people group has only had the scriptures in their language for about 20 years. And from a political standpoint, it was only about fifteen years ago when this territory was filled with communist guerillas. But the area is in peace now, and it's a place where people are receptive to the message of Jesus.

I'll never forget one day when we showed the *Jesus* movie in a difficult-to-reach part of this region. To reach our destination, we drove as far as we could on the local roads. Then, in a drizzle, we hiked about a mile and a half over a rugged trail—carrying our sound, lights, and generators like a pack of human mules. Along the path were several tree bridges consisting of a single log that we had to cross in balance beam fashion. The day was physically grueling, but that night, to see those people watch the *Jesus* movie was all the pay I needed. That joy carried me.

A couple of mornings later, when we were about to leave the region, a man came up to us. "Would several of you come to my village to pray over my son?" he asked. He went on and said, "Last night, when I saw the movie of Jesus, I noticed that Jesus healed a boy that is a lot like my boy. I've spent all my money on witch doctors, and I need help." He told us that his son had these seizures and would fall into the fire, and now he couldn't concentrate enough to go to school.

Our Spanish leader wisely told him, "We can pray for him, but we can do better than that. We can show *you* how to pray for your son just like we can." Within about 30 minutes, the entire family was led to Christ and given a short lesson on how to pray for their son. We prayed, and before we could leave, the man asked a question.

"I really would like for the people of our village to know all this. Would it be possible for one of you to come back and lead us every week in a service in our home?" In about an hour and a half, a house church was born.

The whole morning felt like walking through the pages of the book of Acts and the Bible stories of when the early church was forming. I can attest that there's nothing that compares to the exhilaration of being a part of something that God is doing that will impact lives for all of eternity. Being used by God brought such joy that we didn't view rough conditions and difficulties negatively, but as a vehicle to joy. I've slept on concrete, in flea infested beds, on top of pickup trucks, and endured the rigors of showering and bathing in frigid rivers and streams, and eaten strange things that I've prayed that God would protect me from—not out of a sense of dread, but out of sheer joy! Why? Because I know that the temporary sense of deprivation I go through has a huge joy factor built into it.

You really can handle more than you think you can if you keep your focus on the joy of what God has in store for you. Hang on to it with all you have in times of suffering. Jesus did, and we can too.

There is another angle we need to consider in dealing with our fear of suffering. It comes not in isolation, but in community with others. Paul gives a simple but brilliant picture that captures our imaginations.

Uh oh. I think I see a big eyeball rolling this way.

# Chapter Sixteen: We Want to Pump You Up...

*"Just as each of us has one body with many members, and these members do not all have the same function, so in Christ we who are many form one body, and each member belongs to all the others. We have different gifts, according to the grace given us..."*

— Paul, Romans 12:4-6

Two of my favorite characters on the old Saturday Night Live show were Hans and Franz. Remember them? They'd come out in padded sweat suits, flexing their muscles, imitating Arnold Schwarzenegger chanting, "Ve vant to pump (clap), you up!"

The Apostle Paul loved to talk about the church being a "body." He used this metaphor a lot. And if he were traveling from church to church today, I think he just might put on a padded sweat suit and chant, "Ve vant to pump (clap), you up!" He would like to see people working together in synergy, using their various gifts and talents to encourage one another as they follow Jesus. Check out this animated message of Paul's.

> *A body isn't just a single part blown up into something huge. It's all the different-but-similar parts arranged and functioning together. If Foot said, "I'm not elegant like Hand, embellished with rings; I guess I don't belong to this body," would that make it so? If Ear said, "I'm not beautiful like Eye, limpid and expressive; I don't deserve a place on the head," would you want to remove it from the body? If the body was all eye, how could it hear? If all ear, how could it smell? As it is, we see that God has carefully placed each part of the body right where he wanted it...*

*No part is important on its own. Can you imagine Eye telling Hand, "Get lost; I don't need you"? Or, Head telling Foot, "You're fired; your job has been phased out"? As a matter of fact, in practice it works the other way—the "lower" the part, the more basic, and therefore necessary. You can live without an eye, for instance, but not without a stomach. When it's a part of your own body you are concerned with, it makes no difference whether the part is visible or clothed, higher or lower. You give it dignity and honor just as it is, without comparisons. If anything, you have more concern for the lower parts than the higher. If you had to choose, wouldn't you prefer good digestion to full-bodied hair?*

*The way God designed our bodies is a model for understanding our lives together as a church: every part dependent of every other part... If one part flourishes, every other part enters into the exuberance.*

*You are Christ's body—that's who you are! You must never forget this. Only as you accept your part of that body does your "part" mean anything.*

—Paul, 1 Corinthians 12:12-27 (The Message)

In my profession as a church starter, I have spent a lot of time analyzing what causes churches to grow and how to get new ones started quickly. What I have to say in this chapter may be construed as only applying to churches and church people, but if you think about it, you can see how much of this applies to relationships at work and other places.

For now, let's look deeply into the body life of a church. For starters, I must say that I have grown weary of the ways we complicate the church experience. At the core of a church is not a building, or programs, or a staff, or dynamic services. At the heart of a church are *people* connecting to Jesus and to one another. I've witnessed churches meeting under a tree that had everything they needed, because they had each other. And I've seen churches with massive parking lots and state-of-the-art facilities that are doing a lot of good things but are missing out on the core connection of people to one another that Paul waxed eloquent about. Don't get me wrong, I have nothing against facilities and programs—unless they take away from people connecting with

Jesus and with one another in transformational relationships. Then, I have a problem.

I ache in my soul for people who are attending so many programs that they are running in hyperactive fits to keep up. I feel the isolation that many feel in church services where we are herded in and out of auditoriums and sanctuaries with little connection. I hurt with folks when we go to Bible studies and Sunday Schools where our interactions stay surface level, and we're never given a place to share our hearts with a safe person.

I think that Paul would say that North American Christians have made church way too antiseptic for his taste. I think he'd tell us not to shy away from a little messiness in our relationships and in our church life. Getting involved in other people's lives is at the core of giving and receiving support in a group that is fostering transformational growth in its members. How does all this relate to being transformed in tough times? Glad you asked. In 1 Corinthians 12:26, Paul says...

*If one part suffers, every part suffers with it...*

There are times when you hurt, and I have to carry you. There are times when I hurt, and you have to carry me. Bailing out on one another when times get tough does not produce transformed people.

I like Paul's comedic picture of animated body parts all talking to each other. Using his analogy, I wonder what my body parts might say during a home improvement project where my right hand inadvertently smacked my left thumb with a hammer.

"Hey! That hurts! I'm going to tell the brain what you did to me!" my left thumb hollers.

"Don't do that! I really didn't mean to!" says the right hand, "Besides, it was the arm that swung me around."

"Too late," says my thumb. "I've already alerted the brain. So he already knows."

"We've got a painful situation here between the right hand and the left thumb," says my brain. "Mouth, vocal chords, yell real loud. Left arm, legs, feet, try that new dance move that looks like the funky chicken. Oh, and one more thing, you guys. Try not to say a bad word. You've got a pastor in this body!"

If my body is working right, what is it doing? For the moment, it's focusing on the thumb, trying to take care of it. After my new dance move, I need to evaluate the situation and may wind up putting a band-aid on that thumb, or I might take myself to the doctor—depending on how hurt I think it is.

In the church, the same dynamics are in place. As the church body goes about its life, sometimes accidents and mishaps happen, and people get hurt. I don't see a way around it. To expect a "suffering free" church body is about as unrealistic as expecting to see a "suffering free" human body—especially one that is in the construction business. Why do you suppose the hands of a carpenter or a steel worker or a farmer are so thick and calloused? It's because those hands have been exercised and whacked and hurt and then healed many times as they've been used.

The same is true in the church. We are in the "construction" business. We have our work to do. We are about the business of building up the church. Each of us has a part in the growth, development and expansion of the church. And in doing that work, we get nicked and banged up. This is just part of what should be expected. But do we? Do we expect to be hurt by other people?

The vast majority of us haven't even thought in these terms. When we get hurt in a local church, we want to run to find another church body. We seek one that looks safer than the last one we were in. In extreme situations, that may be a wise move. But in most cases, that's not the answer. A church body, like our own bodies, needs to learn how to look out for and take care of the people-parts who make up that body.

How can a body care for itself? I can think of three ways. Every "body" needs rest, exercise, and good nutrition.

### First, a body needs rest.

One of the Hebrew words for rest is "shabbat"—the word we get "Sabbath" from and a word at the heart of the fourth commandment. In this commandment, God said that He wanted people to work six days and on the seventh to "shabbat" or rest. Once a week, God wants to renew and replenish us.

When we violate the Sabbath principle, we become like little kids who don't want to go to bed at a decent hour, and then when we're cranky the next day we blame everybody else for our problems. A good parent tells a child to go to bed and rest. Our Heavenly Father tells us the same. Some of His children listen and some don't.

Similarly, church bodies need times to rest too. Ever been a part of a hyperactive church that didn't rest? I have. In fact, I've started a couple of them. Because of high expectations and a desire to see our churches grow, it was easy to over program and create systems that burned out our most dedicated people. To the overworked and stressed out church worker, Jesus says...

*"Come to me, all you who are weary and burdened, and I will give you rest. Take my yoke upon you and learn from me, for I am gentle and humble in heart, and you will find rest for your souls. For my yoke is easy and my burden is light." Matthew 11:28-30*

Jesus brings great news to the tired and worn out. And we can learn a lot from the picture Jesus paints here. Let's start with the yoke. Jesus said, "Take my yoke and learn from me." If you're like me, when you hear of a yoke, you might think of a couple of oxen. You might think of how if a yoke is made well and it fits well, the job of the oxen is made easier. But there's more to it than that.

In Jesus' day, and in the culture He was a part of, Jewish Rabbis had an important role in the community. And each Rabbi taught his disciples what he thought was central to understanding and following God. Each of these central teachings was called a "yoke." And most rabbinical "yokes" were nothing more than a series of lists of "do's and don'ts."

One of their highest areas of concern was Sabbath keeping. So they created dozens of Sabbath rules to keep the people from breaking this commandment. It got so anal that on one Sabbath, when Jesus and His disciples were strolling through a wheat field and were popping heads of wheat into their mouths like popcorn (Matthew 12:1-8), the rule keepers (Pharisees) became furious and confronted Jesus. Jesus didn't violate the principle of the Sabbath. He and his disciples were taking it easy. But to some Rabbi, Jesus was violating an important rule.

So when Jesus looked at His followers, who had been blasted for popping wheat into their mouths, He offered some consolation—"My yoke is easy, and My burden is light," He said. "I have come with a yoke—not like the Rabbis around here. I have a yoke that leads to physical and spiritual rest for your souls. Anybody interested?"

And the people raised their hands. "Absolutely!" they said. "We want the kind of rest You're talking about."

## A body also needs exercise.

This may seem contradictory to the Sabbath principle, but it's not. For six days you work; one day you rest. Both work and rest are important. And on the work side of the equation is exercise. Without exercise, our bodies lose their ability to function and move like God designed them to. Muscles atrophy, a "spare tire" grows bigger, and bad things happen to our heart.

In Romans 12, Paul used the body imagery to explain that each of us has different gifts. Then he goes into a heightened sense of urgency, saying that if you have a God-given gift, you need to exercise it in the body. Here's my version of that passage, slightly adapted from the NIV...

> *If you have the gift of prophesying, then prophesy in proportion to your faith. If you have the gift of serving others, then serve somebody! If you have the gift of teaching, then prepare yourself to teach, and get to it! If you have the gift of encouraging, don't hold back, encourage people! If you have the gift of giving, then take that gift seriously and give generously. If you have the gift of leadership, by all means, get in the game right now and lead! If you have the gift of mercy, then show mercy and enjoy every minute that God uses you to offer compassion to others. Romans 12:6-8 (SRV...the Steve Reed Version!)*

By the time Paul gets done with this passage, I picture him in a passionate locker room talk—maybe even standing on the table—

begging anyone who would listen to him to go out and get after their God-given assignment—using their gifts and talents and abilities for the Lord.

Every follower of Christ needs to exercise his or her spiritual gift, not only for the healthy functioning of the church body, but also for the ability to handle difficulties and trials that will inevitably come to that body.

If my body were dangling from a cliff, I'd hope that my hands, feet, and arms were strong enough to help me hang on to the ledge until I could pull myself up to safety. But if none of my body parts had been working out, I'd be a goner. A similar thing is true in our churches. We exercise our gifts to be ready and available to serve the body in times of need as well as times of ease. Exercise is vital.

**A body needs good nutrition.**

A healthy church body, like a healthy physical body, cannot subsist on junk food. You've heard the cliché, "You are what you eat." With regard to church bodies, you might say, "You are what you learn." The church's teachings that are ingested into the body are like the food that will contribute to the health of that body.

We could liken the pastor and teachers to being the primary cooks who serve meals to the church. For many churches, pastors fulfill the role as "head cook." They lead and take responsibility for most of the preaching and teaching. This role of teaching fulfills a vital role, and that role can change as the body grows and develops. Paul wrote the Corinthians (1 Corinthians 3) and said that they were acting like such babies that he needed to put them on an all-milk diet until they grew up. (Bet that didn't exactly read too well to the church there!)

Part of the point made is that teachers need to consider what foods the church body can handle. As a church matures, it can handle more meaty subjects. I've heard Bill Hybels talk about how vital the teaching ministry has been at Willow Creek. When he notices the church struggling in a particular area, he says that a part of the formula for gaining health in that weak area means he and his teaching team will need to address that issue. Getting upset with the flock won't fix the problem, but feeding and leading the church to deal with that issue will help fix the problem.

Still, people complain, and pastors are human too. If you want to raise the blood pressure of a pastor, just go up to one of us and say, "I don't think I'm getting fed around here anymore." If that pastor doesn't deck you on the spot, you're face to face with a spiritual giant!

Rick McGinniss, one of my friends in ministry, told me a line he's always wanted to use when he hears the "I'm not getting fed" complaint from someone. Rick said, "What if you looked them in the eye and asked, 'Are you sure that it's a feeding problem? Looks to me like you need a little exercise.'"

Isn't that good? But it does need a disclaimer like, "Pastors, don't try this at home...this is only for trained professionals or traveling evangelists who can get the heck out of Dodge!"

Being the pastor of a church is tough—especially if you operate as the only "head cook." I believe many of our church bodies are bored because we think that only one person should do all of the cooking. The older I get, the more convinced I am that we need to train a lot more cooks in our congregations. For one, we need to teach church members to be proficient in cooking for themselves. And second, we need to identify and prepare those with teaching gifts to learn how to cook for the whole church body. As more teachers are raised up and released to teach, the body gets a greater variety of food to chew on, and more people get to exercise their gifts.

Often pastors tell me that they could never do team teaching, that only those with large churches and big staffs can do it. I disagree. In many ways I believe it's just the opposite. In larger churches, the quality of the presentation is usually set at a higher level than an entry level person can readily achieve. In a smaller congregation, people are usually more forgiving and open to allow new teachers to teach—especially if they are one of their own. I've discovered that many laymen and laywomen can preach and teach—especially in an area in which they have some experience. If I'm not sure if they can do it on their own, I've actually done dialogue messages where I do a message with one of them. In that scenario, we sit side by side on stools and trade off on points, or I interview them, or I use them to tell a couple of stories. Through the years, I've seen many realize a gift that they never thought they had by offering these kinds of opportunities.

Pastors, if teaching and preaching is killing you, there is a way out. It's called team teaching.

Let's get back to the main road again and talk about suffering and the church body. What are we to do when one member of the body hurts other members? Some leaders are quick to amputate problem people, but for most of us, that seems too drastic. Still, churches often acquire cancerous body parts that need immediate attention—perhaps even chemotherapy sessions or radical surgery.

To talk about this aspect of suffering in the church, I want to change the metaphor and talk about those who can tear up a congregation. I think I can hear them growling now.

# Chapter Seventeen: Sheep Among Wolves...

"Oh Grandmother, what big teeth you have!"

—Little Red Riding Hood

*"I am sending you out like sheep among wolves…"*

—Jesus

*"I am sending you out like sheep among wolves. Therefore be as shrewd as snakes and as innocent as doves. But be on your guard against men; they will hand you over to the local councils and flog you in their synagogues. On my account you will be brought before governors and kings as witnesses to them and to the Gentiles. But when they arrest you, do not worry about what to say or how to say it. At that time you will be given what to say, for it will not be you speaking, but the Spirit of your heavenly Father speaking through you.*

*Brother will betray brother to death, and a father his child; children will rebel against their parents and have them put to death. All men will hate you because of me, but he who stands firm to the end will be saved. When you are persecuted in one place, flee to another. I tell you the truth, you will not finish going through the cities of Israel before the Son of Man comes.*

*A student is not above his teacher, nor a servant above his master. It is enough for the student to be like his teacher, and the servant like his master. If the head of the house has been called Beelzebub, how much more the members of his household!*

*So do not be afraid of them. There is nothing concealed that will not be disclosed, or hidden that will not be made known. What I tell you in the dark, speak in the daylight; what is whispered in your ear, proclaim from the housetops. Do not be afraid of those who kill the body but cannot kill the soul. Rather, be afraid of the One who can destroy both soul and body in hell. Are not two sparrows sold for a penny? Yet not one of them will fall to the ground apart from the will of your Father. And even the very hairs of your head are all numbered. So don't be afraid; you are worth more than many sparrows."*

— Jesus, Matthew 10:16-31

*****************************************************************

I'm not sure I like Jesus' animal metaphors that he uses to describe us, His followers. He sends us out into this world as "sheep among wolves." Why couldn't He have chosen a different analogy? Sheep are not very bright animals. Have you noticed that? They're always getting lost. Don't you wish Jesus had said something like, "I send you as gorillas among chimpanzees—clearly stronger and superior—able to conquer any problem or nuisance that comes along." Or, "I send you as a gazelle among the lions. On most days, you can outrun your hungry adversaries."

No, He says, it's sheep among wolves. Bummer. Jesus might as well have said, "I'm putting you out like a sitting duck in the middle of a bunch of Elmer Fudds crying, 'Oh boy, it's duck season!'"

When attempting to be "sheep among wolves," I think many of us feel more like Daffy Duck and want to cry out, "No, it's wabbit season!" and shift the focus to some "bunny" else. (Bad pun intended.)

What's the point Jesus is making? I think He's trying to tell us that in God's manner of winning the world to Himself, He does it through weakness, not strength—through vulnerability, not defensiveness—through bold openness, not fearful hiddenness. After all, Jesus Himself was "the Lamb slain" on our behalf. So should it surprise us that we might have to follow His example and be His "sheep?"

After starting with the sheep/wolf picture, Jesus changes the slide and shows us another couple of animals. He says we're to be as shrewd as a snake and as harmless or innocent as a dove. What's that about? I think Jesus is telling us to use our heads and to be strategic in what we do. A snake is not fast like a jaguar or mobile like a monkey. So when it captures its target, it has to be able to strategically put itself in a position to strike and get a meal.

But unlike a snake, we're to be innocent like a dove. We're not to manipulate or coerce or attack. We're called to be pure in our motives.

So when we put these metaphors together, what do we have? We are dumb and vulnerable sheep who have a snake-like shrewdness and dove-like innocence.

Most of us can accept the snake and dove correlation, but that sheep thing is still not exactly what we want to hear, is it? Being sent out to be eaten up by wolves is still unappealing no matter how we try to look at it. So, let's ask the question, why would God set us up like this? Why would He let us be so vulnerable?

*I believe it's because ultimately, we're wolf bait.*

Humor me for a minute, and let me go with this. The point of God's redemption is to turn wolves into sheep of His fold. And His strategy for doing that is through us. We are called to be His agents. But it's not going to be done by force or might. It's not going to be done with long teeth or a strong grip. It's not going to be done hiding a dagger under our wool.

God's redemption must be done by way of sacrificial love. It's going to be done with a dependence on the Good Shepherd. It's going to be done with a miraculous infusion of His Spirit into our lives—an infusion of the kind that can turn a wolf into a sheep.

So our job as sheep is to walk with the Shepherd each day—seeking not so much to protect ourselves, but to walk boldly with Him, even if it means following Him into the middle of a pack of wolves who need the Shepherd just like we need the Shepherd.

Jesus' way is the way of suffering. He doesn't sugarcoat this truth for us. He tells it to us straight. But when He tells us difficult things, He also tells us not to play scared. He tells us how much we matter to the Father. He tells us that our God knows the number of hairs on our head—that He's intimately acquainted with every aspect of our lives. Jesus tells us that even sparrows don't fall unnoticed by our God, and since we matter so much more than a small bird, we know that our lives don't go unnoticed by our heavenly Father. He sees and knows the pain and the grief we bear. And better than just knowing about it, He really cares about us as we go through all of it. Knowing this helps us look to heaven and trust God when we're surrounded by what seems like ravenous wolves.

But the wolves "out there" are not always the problem. Sometimes, it's the wolves on the inside that get us most. It's the wolves we sometimes find among the sheep, disguised in sheep costumes. Jesus certainly knows what a wolfy sheep can do. Remember Judas? He was close enough to Jesus to be able to betray him with a kiss on the last night before the crucifixion.

When my dad was working with university students in Lima, Peru, during the early 70's, universities in Latin America were hotbeds for Marxist fervor. Because the government was so concerned about the United States' political influence, they kept a close eye on many missionaries—especially ones working with students. When we were leaving the country, Dad was interrogated at the airport, and in a stunning revelation learned that one of his students was actually a government plant to monitor his activity.

Sometimes a wolfy sheep is not so blatant. Sometimes they are "good" people who turn into enemies in what seems like an irrational instant. What do *you* do when you encounter a "wolfy" sheep? That is a problem, isn't it? Most definitely it's a time to be as wise as a serpent! I think that a "wolfy" sheep can scare us more than the wolves we mingle with in the world. Maybe it's because of the surprise factor—since we're not looking for them and perhaps have our guard down when one day they inadvertently show their fangs.

The truth is, even for most Christians, our wolf nature can come out. We are not perfect, and we are still sinners who can fail God and each other. In church life, wolfy sheep can be lethal to the life and ministry of a local church. When sheep turn into wolves, that's when a church gets into trouble. And undoubtedly, it's a ploy of the evil one to use these situations to thwart God's design and purposes for the church. I know that we could cite shocking stories that would attest to this problem. But here's the deal.

Whether we are in a pack of wolves or surprised by a "wolfy" sheep, our response should be the same. In both cases, we're dealing with the true nature of wolves. And amazingly, our God loves those wolves—so much so that He died for them. And now, Jesus calls us to live as sheep—not stooping to the nature of a wolf, but being wise and strategic as we seek to follow His lead. And as we follow His teachings and His ways—as we learn to live like His sheep—we find that the wolves have no ultimate jurisdiction over our lives. God is still in control. And no matter what we face, we know that we are on the winning team.

One of the best places to see this principle lived out was in the dark days of communist Romania. Let's pull back the iron curtain and take a look.

PART FOUR

# Heroes
## of the
# Suffering Clause

# Chapter Eighteen: Seeds of Greatness...

*"I tell you the truth, unless a kernel of wheat falls to the ground and dies, it remains only a single seed. But if it dies, it produces many seeds."*

— Jesus, John 12:24

*Precious in the sight of the LORD is the death of his saints.*

Psalm 116:15

*"When the perishable has been clothed with the imperishable, and the mortal with immortality, then the saying that is written will come true: 'Death has been swallowed up in victory.' 'Where, O death, is your victory? Where, O death, is your sting?' The sting of death is sin, and the power of sin is the law. But thanks be to God! He gives us the victory through our Lord Jesus Christ."*

— Paul, 1 Corinthians 15:54-57

In 1986, as a seminary student, I attended our denomination's state evangelism conference in Fort Worth, Texas. As is true for most conferences like this, the lineup of speakers was impressive—including many of the superstars that you would probably recognize if I were to mention names. Each was an incredible communicator. But that year one stood out to me above any of the others. His name was Joseph Tson. Joseph was a pastor and leader in the church in Romania.

In those days, Romanian dictator Nicolae Ceausescu still ruled, and communism was still a formidable foe. During his talk, Joseph kept us spellbound as he recounted his experiences of life as a Christian in a communist country. As a pastor, he often became a target for intimidation and interrogation by the authorities. At various times, he endured jail time and beatings.

On one of those occasions when he was arrested and interrogated, the authorities threatened that if he did not cooperate with them, they would kill him.

"Fine," said Joseph. "But realize that I have many cassette tapes of messages out there in the hands of many people. If you kill me, then you will be sprinkling my blood on those tapes, and those who listen to them will think, 'Joseph really must have believed this message so deeply that he was willing to die for it. Maybe I need to seriously consider giving my life to Christ as well.' So, do what you have to do, but understand that if you kill me, it will only spread this message even further."

Joseph said that his interrogators stopped and went to another room. After some time, they came back. "We are not willing to grant your wish to be a martyr," they told him. Later, they released him. Eventually he was given the choice of prison in Romania or exile out of the country. He chose the latter and worked with Radio Free Europe to broadcast encouragement to the people in Romania during those days.

In that message in Fort Worth, Joseph opened his Bible and connected the dots between Jesus' statement that we're sheep among wolves and Jesus' statement that "unless a grain of wheat falls in the ground and dies, it stands alone." Joseph pointed out that the church has always grown from the seeds of the martyrs and from those who are willing to die for their faith. He cited the Apostle Paul, who said that "for me to live is Christ, and to die is gain." He reminded us that according to Jesus, if we choose to save our lives we will lose them, but if we lose our lives for His sake, we will find them.

Even though Joseph was spared, others in Romania were not. In a series of inspiring stories, Chuck Colson reveals the fate of many believers in his book, *The Body*. He highlighted how, in the final days of Ceausescu's reign of terror, many Christians were killed. But as the Christians stood up, so did many in the general populace. In the end, even the soldiers closest to Ceausescu refused to open fire on the protesters. And in a matter of days, Ceausescu was captured. On Christmas day of 1989, he and his wife Elena were executed for crimes against the people.[1]

God does not waste the blood of His martyrs. Those believers in Romania did not die in vain. God used their ultimate sacrifice like a seed planted in the Romanian soil. Today, those seeds are sprouting into a great movement of people coming to Christ.

A similar thing happened to Jim Elliott and his missionary partners who were murdered by the Auca Indians in Ecuador in the 1950's. Today, that tribe is virtually all Christian.

One of the most inspiring things I've ever witnessed happened at a Steven Curtis Chapman concert that my family attended. That night, Steven called up Steve Saint, who is one of the sons of one of the slain missionaries. Steve told the story about his dad, and then he called up a man he called "grandfather." This "grandfather" was actually the Aucan man who killed Steve's father. Yet there they were, arm in arm, telling of the compelling love of Christ that drew this murderer to the Lord, and eventually drew them together.

I'll never forget the image of those two men standing together on that stage. And in a way, it gives me hope that in dealing with the people in my life who may oppose me, or hate me, or ignore me, that God may still have a surprise ending awaiting me if I keep my heart open and ready for reconciliation. Maybe, one day, I'll get to stand arm in arm with those who have hurt me. Maybe I'll get to see how God's resurrection power can be applied to me in my relationships. Maybe His power can be aimed at those who seem so far from God today.

Undoubtedly, it is only through the awesome power of God working through the lives of people that this kind of reconciliation can take place. I am convinced that living out our God-given adventure and planting the seeds of faith in the lives of people is what makes living and dying worth any opposition or persecution that might come.

This way of living can be seen in the lives of those who are listed in what I'd call the Bible's "Suffering Clause Hall of Fame." In fact, let's stop here and take a tour through this "Who's Who" list of those who made it into God's Hall of Champions. As you look at each one, take your time to reflect a little at each exhibit. Each story, each life can teach us something profound. Let's go in.

# Chapter Nineteen: The Suffering Clause
# Hall of Fame...

"You can't get into the hall of fame unless you limp."[1]

—Casey Stengel

*Now faith is being sure of what we hope for and certain of what we do not see. This is what the ancients were commended for...*

*By faith Abel offered God a better sacrifice than Cain did...*

*By faith Enoch was taken from this life, so that he did not experience death...*

*By faith Noah, when warned about things not yet seen, in holy fear built an ark...*

*By faith Abraham, when called to go to a place he would later receive as his inheritance, obeyed and went, even though he did not know where he was going...*

*By faith Abraham, even though he was past age—and Sarah herself was barren—was enabled to become a father...*

*By faith Abraham, when God tested him, offered Isaac as a sacrifice...*

*By faith Isaac blessed Jacob and Esau in regard to their future.*

*By faith Jacob, when he was dying, blessed each of Joseph's sons...*

*By faith Joseph, when his end was near, spoke about the exodus of the Israelites from Egypt and gave instructions about his bones.*

*By faith Moses' parents hid him for three months after he was born...*

*By faith Moses, when he had grown up, refused to be known as the son of Pharaoh's daughter. He chose to be mistreated along with the people of God...*

*By faith the people passed through the Red Sea as on dry land...*

*By faith the walls of Jericho fell, after the people had marched around them for seven days.*

*By faith the prostitute Rahab, because she welcomed the spies, was not killed with those who were disobedient.*

*And what more shall I say? I do not have time to tell about Gideon, Barak, Samson, Jephthah, David, Samuel and the prophets, who through faith conquered kingdoms, administered justice, and gained what was promised; who shut the mouths of lions, quenched the fury of the flames, and escaped the edge of the sword; whose weakness was turned to strength; and who became powerful in battle and routed foreign armies. Women received back their dead... Others were tortured and refused to be released, so that they might gain a better resurrection. Some faced jeers and flogging, while still others were chained and put in prison. They were stoned; they were sawed in two; they were put to death by the sword. They went about in sheepskins and goatskins, destitute, persecuted and mistreated... They wandered in deserts and mountains, and in caves and holes in the ground.*

*These were all commended for their faith, yet none of them received what had been promised. God had planned something better for us so that only together with us would they be made perfect.* Excerpts from Hebrews 11:1-40

\*\*\*\*\*\*\*\*\*\*\*\*\*\*\*\*\*\*\*\*\*\*\*\*\*\*\*\*\*\*\*\*\*\*\*\*\*\*\*\*\*\*\*\*\*\*\*\*\*\*\*\*\*\*\*\*\*\*\*\*\*\*\*\*\*\*\*\*\*\*\*\*\*\*\*\*\*\*\*\*\*\*\*

What's the first thing that pops into your mind when I say, "Cooperstown?" Or, "Canton?" If you are a baseball fan, or a connoisseur of professional football, you know that each is the location of a Hall of Fame. Cooperstown, New York, is the home of baseball's Hall of Fame, and Canton, Ohio, is the home of pro football's Hall of Fame.

Several years ago, the NCAA headquarters was located in a glass and steel high rise near our home in Overland Park, Kansas. (For inquiring minds, the headquarters was relocated to Indianapolis in an irrational move from the heart of the U.S... but I digress!). Inside was a "Hall of Champions" that was open to the public. As you entered into the hall, one of the first things you would notice was the bronze statues and the collages of pictures of NCAA champions in displays all around the room and on the walls. Many athletes were featured, people like swimmer Mark Spitz, basketball coach Jimmy Valvano, Heisman trophy winner Barry Sanders, and hundreds of others.

Several of the exhibits had a "you are there" feel to them. One had astroturf and a 360-degree picture of a crowd in the stands that surrounded you. With a push of a button, you could hear the sights and sounds of being at midfield for a coin toss before a college football game.

In writing this chapter, I began to wonder about how many sports "Halls of Fame" exist. I assumed that there might be a dozen or so. So I hopped on the internet to see what I could find out. I was overwhelmed!

In a few clicks, I discovered dozens of the sports versions, finding a Hall of Fame for just about every sport imaginable—even badminton! But I quickly discovered that many other kinds of Halls of Fame exist. There are many different music Halls of Fame. I was already aware of the Rock and Roll Hall of Fame in Cleveland and the Country Music Hall of Fame in Nashville. But those were just two of the dozens that are out there. I found that virtually every genre of music has its official Hall of Fame.

Besides music Halls of Fame, you can find hundreds of other types. There are Halls of Fame for teachers, business leaders, broadcasters, inventors, scientists, writers, environmentalists, economists, cowboys, cartoonists, conservative politicians, chess players, artists, aviators, astronauts, advertisers, farmers, lawyers, mechanics, miners, snow mobilers, jugglers, dancers, physicians, photographers, quilters, and streakers! There are even Halls of Fame for nonhumans. Included in these are Halls for horses, dogs, cats, and even sharks! Or was that included in the Hall for lawyers? There is even a Hall of Fame for left-handed DNA! I'm not making this up.

Amazingly, hundreds of museums and places exist to honor outstanding people and achievements. And as interesting as those hallowed places can be, for me, none of them compare to actually being in the presence of the true greatness of a living legend. People who attest to this might cite meeting Nelson Mandela, or Billy Graham, or Mother Theresa.

Mike Evans, a minister and TV producer, tells of one such occasion in a recent book, *The Unanswered Prayers of Jesus*. While in the airport in Rome, he happened to cross paths with Mother Teresa. She had just come from a trip to the United States, and Mike asked her how it was—mentioning that she must be sad to return to the suffering people of India after enjoying the comforts of the United States for a short time.

"No, no," she responded. "It is in the United States that I am sad. I believe that it is the poorest country on earth."

Mike gave her a puzzled look and asked, "But why?"

"Ah," she went on. "The United States is poor in spirit, and that is the worst kind of poverty."[2]

Only someone with a wisdom forged in the sufferings of people all over the world could glean such insight. Helmut Thielicke, a famous German pastor and theologian, is reported to have made a similar statement after touring across the United States. He was asked what might be the greatest deficiency among American Christians, and he replied, "They have an inadequate view of suffering."[3] Could it be that the material possessions that we use to cushion our current existence are keeping us from experiencing a richness of the soul that Mother Teresa and Helmut Thielicke noticed more readily in Christians in other parts of the world?

For me, true heroes of character inspire me most. I love drinking from the wisdom of those who have lived well—who by virtue of their character or their commitments to noble ideals, even in spite of great adversity and under difficult circumstances, have inspired us to pattern our own lives after theirs.

One such hero for me is Dr. Carl Hunker. Dr. Hunker was a missionary to China shortly before the communists took over and ousted the missionaries. Now in his 90's, Dr. Hunker claims to be retired, but that is clearly a misnomer for a man who has done more ministry in his "retirement" than many of us do in a lifetime. He has continued to start ministries and Bible studies and churches for the Chinese people to this day.

One day, Dr. Hunker invited me to come over to his home in Liberty, Missouri, for a chance to go out to lunch. When I walked into his home, I noticed some of his Chinese art and pictures. I asked about several of the items, and one question led to another. Soon I was enthralled with Dr. Hunker's stories.

At one point I asked Dr. Hunker about the circumstances surrounding his family having to evacuate their home and leave China. "Oh my, that will take a while to tell you that story," he replied.

"I've got all day," I said.

"Are you sure?"

"As long as you don't kick me out, I'll be here listening."

With that, Dr. Hunker sat down and told me about how he and his wife had spent years praying and preparing to be missionaries to China. After two years of language study, they arrived at their assigned city in China. They made friends and began their work with the churches. The day Dr. Hunker preached his first sermon in Chinese, one of the other missionaries in his mission came to him.

"Carl, I need to speak with you," he said.

Hearing a tone of concern in his voice, Dr. Hunker replied, "What's the matter?"

"The communists are within days of taking over this city," he informed. "All of our mission personnel need to get packed up and go."

"But we just got here this year," Dr. Hunker countered. "Can't we wait it out?"

"It's too dangerous. You must go."

So they packed their things and arranged to take a train out. When they got to the train station, thousands of people were crowded around trying to get on trains to leave the city. When Dr. Hunker and his wife got on the train, they turned to wave goodbye, and then realized something terrible had happened.

"I thought my wife had our infant daughter and she thought I had her," Dr. Hunker explained. "She was still in the arms of one of our Chinese friends. As the train began to move, there was no way to get off the train because of all the people crowded around us. So our friends took action. They passed our baby over the heads of everyone and into the waiting arms of my wife."

During that day, Dr. Hunker told me of how they regrouped and moved to Taiwan, where he helped start hundreds of churches and became the president of a seminary there in Taiwan. He told of touching moments with his wife who battled bravely with cancer before succumbing to it over 20 years ago.

That whole day, I was in awe, because I knew that I was in the presence of true greatness. As I write these words, I know that Dr. Hunker would wince at my assessment of him. And that's what makes him so great. Dr. Hunker is the epitome of a humble man who is finishing well the race God marked out for him.

A few years ago, I spent a couple of days with him when attending our state convention meetings. We decided to carpool to the meeting and share a hotel room. For some reason, we got the time down wrong and arrived two hours early. Dr. Hunker asked me, "Do you need to make some phone calls and do some work?"

"No, I've set aside this time to spend with you."

"Okay," he said, "then let's pray."

We then experienced a wonderful time of prayer together. Dr. Hunker didn't think a thing about it. Prayer is so much a part of who he is that he defaults there almost automatically. As we prayed, he moved me to want to pray like him. His simple act motivated me more than attending 25 lectures on how to pray. We just prayed. And I was changed.

Greatness can be seen in the lives of many in our world. But true greatness is not always visible to the casual observer. To spot it, you have to pay attention to what God sees and not what men see. God knows where to find true greatness. Jesus said, "The greatest among you will be your servant." In God's eyes, greatness comes in moments of "hiddenness"—not visibility. Greatness comes in staying faithful long past the due dates and time frames of human understanding.

In God's eyes, there is one thing that distinguishes a man or woman for His Hall of Fame. What is it? It's faith. It's not intelligence or beauty or social status or talents or abilities in certain areas. It is faith.

To highlight this, the author of the book of Hebrews gives us a list of people who qualify for God's Hall of Fame. It's found in Hebrews 11, and it's what we read at the beginning of this chapter. While some of it may make for slow reading, it's worth not rushing past. In fact, let's take a slower walk through the Hall here, and observe some of the exhibits highlighting the lives of some amazing people.

As we begin our tour, we see an exhibit for Enoch, who lived a long and Godly life—having a life-transforming experience after the birth of his son Methuselah. Then we come upon a larger display—this one for Noah, who after over 120 years was vindicated for his faithfulness to build the ark, and he and his family was saved from the flood. Around the corner is Abraham. This exhibit takes up some space. Here we see a map and pictures detailing his great move from his homeland to the land of Canaan. In a prominent spot, we see a picture of Isaac, as a happy little boy. Underneath the picture is the story of Isaac's miracle birth in Abe's old age, and how this birth fulfilled the first part of God's promise that through him would come many descendants. Speaking of his descendants, as we move past Abraham's section, there's space given to Isaac, Jacob, and to Joseph.

Joseph's exhibit is one of the most striking. His father babied and catered to him in his younger years, but after being sold into slavery by his brothers, he endured incredible hardships and mistreatment for much of his life—eventually experiencing vindication from God.

In a separate section, we find a big display of maps and events highlighting the life of Moses. Moses chose to be mistreated along with his people over living the opulent lifestyle of a prince in Pharaoh's household. Then we read of the subsequent victories for Israel after Moses died.

Over in the corner, nearly out of sight, is an interesting plaque dedicated to Rahab, the prostitute. No pictures are given, so prudence must have prevailed. She made it because God used her to spare the lives of many Jewish people.

Down the way, we see Gideon, who rose up from cowardice to become a military hero. Then we find Barak, who teamed with Deborah to lead a mighty victory over their enemies during the period of the judges. Right next to Barak's spot is Samson's. Though he yo-yoed his whole life, he came back in a bittersweet victory over his captors when he brought the house down.

Admittedly some of these exhibits are confusing. Jephthah's exhibit required deeper reading. He was a great military leader who led the people of Israel in some stunning victories. But before one of those victories, he vowed to sacrifice whatever he saw first when he got home—should God grant the victory. Unfortunately the first person he saw when entering his home was his only daughter. And to keep his word, he sacrificed her. Was this a lesson in not making foolish vows, or in keeping your word? I don't know. But Jephthah's faith was notable nonetheless.

David has one of the biggest displays—rising from a slingshot-slinging, harp-playing shepherd boy to become king of Israel and dubbed "a man after God's own heart."

Rounding out those mentioned by name in this Hall of Fame is the prophet Samuel, and many of the other prophets who persevered through many difficult circumstances to keep pointing Israel back to God.

But we're not done yet. In the middle of everything is an area that is roped off. Prominently placed on a pillar is a limestone tablet. Chiseled in the stone it reads, "Those vindicated by God in heaven." Below that heading are the words from Hebrews 11.

*... Others were tortured and refused to be released, so that they might gain a better resurrection. Some faced jeers and flogging, while still others were chained and put in prison. They were stoned; they were sawed in two; they were put to death by the sword. They went about in sheepskins and goatskins, destitute, persecuted and mistreated—the world was not worthy of them. They wandered in deserts and mountains, and in caves and holes in the ground. These were all commended for their faith, yet none of them received what had been promised. God had planned something better for us so that only together with us would they be made perfect. Hebrews 11:35-40*

What is this exhibit all about? It seems to be something akin to a Christian tomb of an unknown soldier. This exhibit proclaims that there are those who are not vindicated in this life for their faithful deeds. Some see parts of God's promises fulfilled in their lifetimes, while others are only vindicated in heaven.

Abraham was promised many descendants, a land, and that one of his descendants would bless the world. He only saw the beginnings of each fulfilled. Moses saw many miraculous things, but he died before the Israelites reached the Promised Land.

God's Hall of Fame includes many who never received a plaque or trophy in this life, but who will get a huge reception in the banquet halls of heaven. And throughout the centuries, God is still taking inductees into this part of the Hall. People like Martin and Gracia Burnham or Jim and Elisabeth Elliot. Some die prematurely, and some live and love a little longer than many before passing their torch of faith to others. Thousands upon thousands of people will be given some space in the Halls of Heaven. And what's exciting is that you and I have an opportunity to live our lives in such a faithful and wholehearted way that we can join our heroes of the faith some day.

You and I can live our lives like our heroes. But to do so, we'll have to be open to the possibility that perhaps we might not receive vindication for our faithfulness on this earth. If Hebrews 11 is any indicator, we may not see our God-given dreams fulfilled here. Some of us will only see vindication from the grandstands of heaven.

And this is a place where getting in touch with the suffering clause is our only option. Our lives are truly in God's hands, and to fight this part of suffering is one that will only delay our joy in the moments we have right now.

As I write these words, I think again of my friend, Curtis Sergeant, who I mentioned earlier in the book, who has witnessed the incredible faith of Chinese believers. Many of them have nothing to hang on to except this one promise—that maybe they get to be a part of the group that is vindicated in heaven. Many of them don't even think in terms of vindication on earth. They know that they will be poured out like a drink offering for God—perhaps dying in a seemingly senseless way. Yet, if church history is any indication, no person's sacrifice for Christ is a waste. Often, believers and non-believers alike will see the true commitment of their fallen friend or brother and decide to pick up their own torch of faith and carry it past what the original bearers of that torch could have imagined.

God has the last word in the end. We can live faithful lives right now—even when we see no apparent vindication coming to us in this life. We can look to the exhibit of "Those Vindicated in Heaven," and trust that God hasn't missed us in the shuffle of our brief history on this earth. God can be trusted with our lives and any legacy that may follow us.

Isn't that good news? Isn't that freeing? Yet, as inspirational as this thought is for us right now, I wonder if some among us—maybe even you—truly desire to hold a high and noble view on suffering, but the pain of your situation clouds your every waking thought. You may have even picked up this book for perspective on your intense pain and found that while this book has been good for inspiration and perspective, you still can hardly see straight because your pain is so great. If that describes you, I'd like to slow down a minute, give you a warm embrace, take you by the hand, and walk with you for a few chapters as you consider your options in the way you view and respond to your own pain and suffering.

I want to take you over to the home of a remarkable lady who can identify with the problems of physical pain that you may be facing at this very moment.

# BOOK II

# TRANSFORMED

# BY

# TOUGH TIMES

*"I have fought the good fight, I have finished the race, I have kept the faith."*
 — **The Apostle Paul, 2 Timothy 4:7**

# Chapter Twenty: The Suffering Clause Hall of Pain...

"Some of His children must go into the furnace to testify that the Son of God is there with them."[1]

—Elizabeth Payson Prentiss

*"Why is my pain unending and my wound grievous and incurable?"*
—Jeremiah, Jeremiah 15:18

*"May you be able to feel and understand, as all God's children should, how long, how wide, how deep, and how high his love really is; and to experience this love for yourselves, though it is so great that you will never see the end of it or fully know or understand it. And so at last you will be filled up with God himself."*

— Paul, Ephesians 3:18 (The Living Bible)

*Precious in the sight of the LORD is the death of his saints.*
Psalm 116:15

*"When the perishable has been clothed with the imperishable, and the mortal with immortality, then the saying that is written will come true: 'Death has been swallowed up in victory.' 'Where, O death, is your victory? Where, O death, is your sting?' The sting of death is sin, and the power of sin is the law. But thanks be to God! He gives us the victory through our Lord Jesus Christ."*

— Paul, 1 Corinthians 15:54-57

In the previous chapter I talked about "The Hall of Fame." In this chapter, I want to talk about "The Hall of Pain." This is the place for those who are enduring suffering and who aren't in a position to accept glib, easy answers to their pain. In fact, for the next few chapters, I'd like to address those who are in the middle of suffering. Perhaps your pain is too great for you to feel like debating the finer points of theology or pondering the depths of your suffering.

Such was the situation of my mother, Wanda Reed. Nineteen years ago, Mom, a schoolteacher at the time, hurt her back putting books away on the last day of school. That "muscle pull" led to other aches, and she began to have chronic pain. It wouldn't go away. She went to one doctor after another, and none helped her. After two years of constant probing and tests and not getting an answer, one doctor told her that she needed to see a psychiatrist, because the pain was all in her head.

"I'm willing to see a psychiatrist to help me cope with the pain," my mother cried. "But I know it's not just in my head. I know I'm not crazy. I may not be thinking straight right now, but I'm not crazy!"

After more than $1,000,000 of misdiagnosis and medical bills, a doctor finally discovered she had Lyme disease. Mom was right. It wasn't all in her head. But now, even with a proper diagnosis, Mom had a long and uncertain road to travel to seek to regain her health. There were no magic pills to take. No guaranteed, easy steps to reclaim what she'd lost. It was a grueling, painful regimen of experimentation with high powered antibiotics and pain management—lasting over 5 years. At the worst of it, she was confined to a couch for about three or four years—only getting out when Dad took her to one of her many doctor appointments.

Little by little, through a combination of medicine, nutrition, physical therapy, and boatloads of prayer, she started reclaiming her life. Later, she got to a point where she could drive, run errands, putter around in her garden, take long trips, and enjoy spoiling her grandkids. Eleven years ago, when Mom was doing quite a bit better, but still relatively fresh from some of the most painful parts of her experience, I asked her to give me some advice to pass on to those who experience chronic pain. Sitting on the couch that was her bed for years, Mom began to hand me her handwritten notes, and then she told me some of her thoughts. We talked and I scribbled much of this down on a notepad, and now I would like to pass her insights on to you. Here are some of Mom's thoughts that might encourage you while enduring some painful times.

## WHAT TO DO WHEN ENDURING PAINFUL TIMES:

### 1. LIVE ONE MINUTE AT A TIME.

Mom told me that when she was in constant pain, the mental battle was intense. She couldn't think about lasting the next 10 minutes, much less a whole day. "It was too overwhelming to think about months or years down the road," she said. "All I could do was take everything one minute at a time."

Mom talked about how she often prayed, "God, help me in the next 10 minutes to relax. She'd then take it a minute at a time until she got through 10 minutes. Then she'd pray, "Lord help me go another 10 minutes." Minute by minute, she'd make it through a day.

She also talked about how music and scriptures were so important to her during her most painful days. To cope, Mom collected scripture promises from the Bible. She wrote out notes to herself on index cards and would read those cards often. During a time when she had to lay on her stomach for extended periods of time, she read those scriptures aloud into a tape recorder. Later, when she could not flip through her cards, she would play back that tape so that she could continue to saturate her spirit with scriptures like Matthew 6:34...

> So don't be anxious about tomorrow. God will take care of your tomorrow too. Live one day at a time.
> Matthew 6:34 (Living Bible)

Mom told how some of her toughest times came through many dark and lonely nights when the pain kept her from sleeping. When she felt that she didn't even have the mental energy to pray, she turned on her inspirational music or her homemade tape recordings. Often, she'd pray, "Lord, I can't even think straight to pray, so let this tape express my prayer to You."

## 2. REMEMBER THAT GOD HAS A REASON AND A PURPOSE FOR YOUR LIFE.

Another thing that Mom mentioned over and over was that it was hard to keep perspective when she saw no apparent purpose to her suffering. And so she talked a lot about how in spite of the fact that the circumstances don't always make sense, God still has a purpose for our lives. She clung to the promises that one day she'd know the purpose behind her pain. Often in the middle of her pain, when she saw no end in sight, Mom would pray, "God, if I could just see a reason or a purpose I'd be able to make it. I need to know that You still have hope for me." Some days all she had to cling to were words like from Jeremiah…

> *For I know the plans I have for you says the Lord. They are plans for good and not for evil, to give you a future and a hope. Jeremiah 29:11 (Living Bible)*

Now that she's lived through much of this, she can see a greater purpose, but during the darkest days, all she had to go on was that God would make good on His promise and nothing else.

## 3. VISUALIZE FUTURE JOY.

Mom took vacations and trips in her mind to favorite places in Colorado and New Mexico. While working through her daily regimen of physical therapy exercises, she tried to engage her mind in productive thoughts. Looking to future joy was important.

I mentioned earlier in the book that Jesus endured the cross by focusing on the future joy that would come. Mom picked up on this, and in her own handwriting showed me this verse…

> *Let us fix our eyes on Jesus, the author and perfecter of our faith, who for the joy set before him endured the cross, scorning its shame, and sat down at the right hand of the throne of God. Consider him who endured such opposition from sinful men, so that you will not grow weary and lose heart. Hebrews 12:2-3*

Mom said that if Jesus needed to look ahead to future joy to endure the cross, maybe it was a good mental exercise for her to do as well.

### 4. SURROUND YOURSELF WITH ENCOURAGING PEOPLE WHO CARE.

At one point in my interview with my mother, I asked the question, "Where was God in your hurt?"

"In family and friends," she said.

She talked about my son Josh who had a knack for cheering her up when few could. She continued, "I remember when Josh was three or four years old. One day he said, 'Mimi, if you don't feel like praying anymore, that's okay, lots of people are praying for you. You just take it easy!'"

Mom saw God's hand in the friends who encouraged her and listened to her and loved her. She also talked about having to overlook the misguided friends who offered all kinds of remedies and pieces of advice like, "If you just had enough faith, you'd get well." She talked about my dad sticking by her.

As Mom listed all the people who encouraged her, the thought hit me that sometimes you and I are God's representatives to make His presence real to someone in pain. Jesus' words in Matthew came to me…

> I was sick and you looked after me…whatever you did for one of the least of these…you did it for me." Matthew 25:36, 40

I've always seen this verse in the context of doing our deeds for the "least of these" because it could be that we're doing a good deed for Jesus without knowing it. But I wonder if this also works in reverse. To the one suffering, I am Jesus to them!

What's the common denominator on both sides of this equation? It's Jesus! He's identifying with the helpless in their suffering, and He's ministering through the presence of His follower who gets the privilege of being "Jesus with skin on" to that one who suffers.

During our lifetimes, we have occasions to be on both sides of this. Sometimes we get to serve the suffering in Jesus' name, and sometimes we get to be the suffering one who others serve as they would Jesus in disguise.

When Mom was in a hospital to receive physical therapy during her recovery, she had to attend some group therapy sessions as a part of her treatments. In Mom's group were a couple of people whom she absolutely could not stand. They were obnoxious. They were profane. She hated being around them. Every moment spent near those people was as torturous as the physical therapy she was enduring.

But she couldn't avoid them and fully participate in her physical treatments and group sessions, so finally, out of self defense, she prayed, "God, help me see these people the way You see them." Not long after that, she learned more about one of the men that grated on her nerves. This man was a big, tough looking guy with tattoos all over his arms. He told the group during one of their sessions that he once worked on power lines. One day, he was working on one of the lines that went over one of the bridges that cross the Missouri river north of downtown Kansas City when he and a partner fell. His partner died. But somehow, he had been miraculously rescued.

He said that as he was sinking to the bottom of the river, he figured he was going to die, and he heard a voice as plain as day talking to him. He knew no one was around him, so it baffled him. At that point, Mom asked him, "You think it might have been God?"

He thought a minute and said, "You know, it might have been."

Mom said that understanding this man's story gave her enormous compassion for him, and in the days that followed, she actually looked forward to seeing the other difficult people. Toward the end of her stay there, she gave this man some literature about how to have a relationship with God. He took it and said that he would give it serious consideration. A few minutes later, she noticed this tough guy sitting in a corner reading her gift and weeping. Mom then said, "I probably won't know for sure on this side of heaven, but sometimes I wonder if part of my purpose in my pain had something to do with what God wanted me to do for that man."

What's interesting to me is that in her pain, Mom still had an internal compass that pointed her toward helping others. Something inside led her to a belief that she mustn't "waste" her pain when it could be used to help someone else. So one of the things that helped my Mom cope was the thought that one day she would get to help another hurting person. And when she began to look at people the way God sees them, she was better prepared to help others—even in the middle of her own severe pain.

### 5. GIVE GOD YOUR WORRIES.

Mom discovered that many things in our lives are beyond our control. Yet it is easy for us to spend time worrying about areas we can't do much about. This verse was another of her favorites...

*Let Him (God) have all your worries and cares, for He is always thinking about you and watching everything that concerns you. 1 Peter 5:7 (Living Bible)*

You have to know my mom, but we lovingly have called her a "professional worrier." She's good at it! And she has worried and fussed over us kids and her grandkids for years. For her, giving God her worries had to become a discipline. Over and over, many times a day, Mom offered up her worries to God. She knew that she couldn't handle them, and this verse was her reminder that God cared and was on the job to attend to her concerns.

As I left Mom's house, I felt that I had been given a gift. I felt that I was receiving a priceless legacy of stories that I needed to pass on to my children. And I walked away with some helpful and practical things to offer those who don't need easy answers to their pain.

One question still lingered for me that I had asked my mother. She answered it with a response of faith, but not all would have answered the question like she did. The question? "Where is God when we hurt?"

With all due respect to Philip Yancey, who wrote one of the most helpful and classic books on pain and suffering that bears this title, I want to be so bold as to offer an answer to that question. Let's head over to the chalkboard, so I can scribble out some of my thoughts.

129

# Chapter Twenty-one: Where is God When it Hurts?

*The LORD is close to the brokenhearted and saves those who are crushed in spirit.* Psalm 34:18

*God has said, "Never will I leave you; never will I forsake you."* Hebrews 13:5

*Where can I go from your Spirit? Where can I flee from your presence? If I go up to the heavens, you are there; if I make my bed in the depths, you are there. If I rise on the wings of the dawn, if I settle on the far side of the sea, even there your hand will guide me, your right hand will hold me fast. If I say, "Surely the darkness will hide me and the light become night around me," even the darkness will not be dark to you; the night will shine like the day, for darkness is as light to you. For you created my inmost being; you knit me together in my mother's womb. I praise you because I am fearfully and wonderfully made; your works are wonderful, I know that full well.* Psalm 139:7-14

When it comes to answering the question, "Where is God when it hurts?" I believe there are only five categories of answers that we can choose from. As I list these, remember that you will have to choose what you believe, so weigh these options carefully.

## WHERE IS GOD WHEN IT HURTS?

### 1. GOD IS NOWHERE.

This view says that God doesn't exist. So if God doesn't exist, our question, "Where is God when it hurts?" is irrelevant, because we're asking a fairytale question that can't be answered in a real world without a God.

God is considered a conceptual idea, but not a reality. This position expresses the view of an atheist.

### 2. God is up in heaven, but He doesn't get involved in earthly stuff.

In this view, God wound the world up like a clock and has stepped away to let it run on its own. He is not particularly worried or concerned with me or my hurts, so I'm really on my own. This is the position of a deist.

### 3. God is close by, but He is an angry, malicious God.

In this view, God inflicts pain on us for every little thing we do wrong. No bad deed goes unpunished, and no good deed seems to make much difference. Marcion, an early church leader who was excommunicated in 144 A.D., saw the Old Testament God this way and distinguished Him from the loving God of the New Testament.[1]

From a philosophical view, if you push this view of a malicious God to an extreme, where he punishes people for even the good deeds they do, then you have come up with a "god" that is more like a devil—seeking only to hurt human beings.

### 4. God is close by and wants the best for us, but He can't do anything about it.

In this view, God is a loving but weak God. He wants to be involved in our lives and make a difference in our situation on earth, but is powerless to do so. Put more crassly, God is nice, but He's a wimp. So we are here on earth to fend for ourselves, while God cheers for us on the sidelines.

This idea fits in the category of existential philosophies of the past century. In an existential view of God, His presence is irrelevant to our human predicament, and therefore people need to seek answers elsewhere.

**5. GOD IS CLOSE BY AND IS BOTH WILLING AND ABLE TO HELP US IN OUR PAIN.**

In this view, God is a good God. And He can make a genuine difference in what happens to us when we suffer.

With these five options out on the table, let's take a look at each of them just for a minute. I won't be able to go into great depth, but for each I will offer my own view and hope to offer you some resources about where to look for further help in sorting through these options for yourself.

**Let's look at the first option—that God does not exist.** For me, this view doesn't even seem plausible. I can't even imagine not believing in an all-powerful God as described in the Bible. Either God exists or nothing else makes sense.

Yet, just because I am a gung-ho believer in God should not cause me to gloss over the deep questions of one who wonders about this issue. If that is where you are in your journey, I'd highly recommend Lee Strobel's book *The Case for a Creator*. Strobel, a former legal journalist for the *Chicago Tribune*, and former atheist, offers his unique perspective on the matter and gives a well thought out and reasoned approach for believing in God.

**For the second option—that God is distant but unconcerned about me**, I've had a hard time buying this one. As I read the Bible, I read of a God Who is much closer than that. Let's take a look at one of the verses from the Bible that we read at the beginning of the chapter…

*The LORD is close to the brokenhearted and saves those who are crushed in spirit. Psalm 34:18*

When I read that, it blows the distant God theory for me. Yet, I can hear some spiritual seekers say, "Steve, wait a minute. This is all fine and dandy for you to say, but what if I don't believe the Bible? Aren't there errors in the Bible? If so, why should I believe this verse you've given me?"

Fortunately (in my opinion) here's another instance where the experts like Lee Strobel come to our rescue. Lee's book, *A Case for Christ,* has some interesting and informative chapters detailing his own hard-nosed investigation into the reliability of the Bible. If you struggle with this, I'd recommend Strobel to you again.

**For the third option—that God is punishing,** Jesus faced this view head on when His disciples walked along and saw a blind man. They figured his blindness was caused by somebody's sin. Let's read about it...

> *As he went along, he saw a man blind from birth. His disciples asked him, "Rabbi who sinned, this man or his parents, that he was born blind?" "Neither this man nor his parents sinned," said Jesus, "but this happened so that the work of God might be displayed in his life....Having said this, he spit on the ground, made some mud with the saliva, and put it on the man's eyes. "Go," he told him, "wash in the pool of Siloam" (this word means Sent). So the man went and washed, and came home seeing.*
>
> John 9:1-3, 5-7

Clearly, Jesus Himself eliminated this option. People don't necessarily get sick because they have sinned. Disease and sickness can happen to anyone. Yet Jesus and the Father care and are able to heal. We'll come back to this view in further chapters, but for now let's set it aside.

**For the fourth option—that God is loving but a wimp.** Again, I must go to the Bible. Paul tells us this...

> *Now to him who is able to do immeasurably more than all we ask or imagine, according to his power that is at work within us, to him be glory in the church and in Christ Jesus throughout all generations, for ever and ever! Amen. Ephesians 3:20-21*

For Paul, there was no doubt that he served a God Who was more powerful than we can even imagine. And Paul did not speculate this on the basis of a theory, but on seeing God move in his own life and ministry. A look at the book of Acts is all it takes to see why Paul would see God as an all-powerful being.

For me, all I need is a look at the resurrection. Jesus' death on the cross was the most loving act in history. Then His resurrection proved that God could do something about death. If God can pull off resurrections, surely He is able to handle my problems. So this view of an impotent God doesn't hold up for me either. And that leads us to our final option…

**God is close, and He is willing and able to help us.** You know me well enough by now to know that this is the option that I believe based on what the Bible has to say, based on my own experience, and based on the insights and experiences of others I know.

I believe that God is able to do immeasurably more than I can think or imagine (Ephesians 3:20). I believe that God wants to do something positive in my life. But I also admit to the fact that pain still exists. It's undeniable. So the natural question is, "How can God be close and there still be pain in my life?" He ought to drive out the pain when I have it. Shouldn't He?

Well, maybe He should if *we* were to call the shots. But we don't. Let's revisit another verse that I highlighted at the beginning of this chapter.

> *God has said, "Never will I leave you; never will I forsake you."* Hebrews 13:5

We rant and rave and beg God to take away our pain, while God offers us an unshakable promise that is not dependent on our pain. We want a Genie-like God granting our wishes. We want ease and comfort. Yet God does not promise the absence of pain but that He will be *with us* in the middle of our pain. God's offer to us is profound and personal, because He offers Himself and His presence.

In a time of crisis, what is God's presence worth? What is His strength, and His love, and His compassion worth? Could it be, that when we ask for pain removal, we ask for too little? Could it be that God, in His infinite wisdom, offers us something better? Could it be that we are missing out on joy and deep fulfillment in our lives, because we aren't paying attention to His presence when we hurt?

As we ponder these questions about God, we need to address something that might challenge our view of pain. To talk about it, we need to take a trip to a leper colony with Dr. Paul Brand and learn from an amazing and caring physician who has dedicated his life to people who suffer from a debilitating and humiliating disease.

# Chapter Twenty-two: Pain, the Gift Nobody Wants...

"Pain is God's megaphone to rouse a deaf world."[1]

—C.S. Lewis

In the book titled *Pain, The Gift Nobody Wants,* Dr. Paul Brand (with help from Philip Yancey) tells about his life in treating leprosy patients in India, England, and the United States. In the book, Dr. Brand states that he could cure leprosy if he could get his patients to experience one sensation. Pain. Because those who suffer from leprosy feel no pain, they do damage to their bodies when no automatic pain mechanisms go off to alert them to stop hurting themselves.

One story highlights this problem. It's the story of a mother and her little girl named Tanya. The first year, Tanya seemed to be a healthy child. But one day, when Tanya was 18 months old, everything changed. The mother came in to check on Tanya playing in her playpen and found that there were bloody swirls on the white plastic sheets. In her own words, the mother said, "I didn't grasp the situation at first, but when I got closer I screamed. It was horrible. The tip of Tanya's finger was mangled and bleeding, and it was her own blood she was using to make those designs on the sheets.

"I yelled, 'Tanya, what happened!' She grinned at me, and that's when I saw the streaks of blood on her teeth. She had bitten off the tip of her finger and was playing in the blood."[2]

From that point on, this mother watched the debilitation of her little girl. Doctors like Dr. Brand did their best to help, but they were limited in what they could do. Why? Because they didn't have the ability to help Tanya feel any pain.

Multiply that story by the hundreds and thousands of patients that Dr. Brand saw in his lifetime, and we get an understanding of why Dr. Brand calls pain a "gift." It is a gift to us, a warning signal that something is wrong and we need to do something to care for ourselves. Without it, we can do horrible, irreversible damage and not even realize we've hurt ourselves in awful, grotesque ways. In fact, Dr. Brand often exclaims, "Thank God for pain!"[3]

Contrast this attitude to that of most of us in the United States, who are so intolerant of experiencing pain of any kind that we've fueled the $63 billion a year pain relief industry that proclaims such slogans as, "I haven't got time for the pain."[4] Dr. Brand sees most Americans as having suffered less than the rest of the world because of our relative ease and comforts of life, but at the same time we are afraid of that suffering more than any people he has worked with in the world.[5]

With Dr. Brand's view that physical pain is a "gift," I wonder if the same might be true of emotional and relational pains as well. Could our pains of various kinds help us more than we can know right now?

C.S. Lewis, who I quoted at the beginning of this chapter, was one of the most brilliant thinkers and writers of the last generation. He often spoke of how pain and suffering can contribute to maturity. According to Lewis, without pain, we'd still be playing with toys in the nursery. Like toddlers, we'd never develop a sense of balance and learn to walk without experiencing the pain of falling. Pain helps us make better decisions. Pain helps us take corrective action that will benefit us in the future.[6]

As I've worked on this book, one thing has become abundantly clear to me. I find few among us who are very discerning when it comes to figuring out our pain and suffering. Often we can come up with the most illogical conclusions when we hurt. And when we evaluate our pain, we tend to overestimate our own pain and inconvenience when comparing it to the pains of others.

As I was writing the first edition of this book, a friend met me for a prayer time. He was 15-20 minutes late and apologized, citing an unusual traffic jam. On the radio he heard about a school bus accident, but details were sketchy. We prayed, and then later in the day learned that this school bus, carrying 53 children, had lost control—becoming a deadly missile, crashing through a busy intersection. Two people were killed, and several others—mostly children, were seriously injured. My friend commented that now he felt guilty for the irritation he felt when he was inconvenienced by the delay.

This incident highlights how perspective changes everything. Without a proper perspective, we can be petty and selfish, but with an accurate picture of reality, we can respond better to our pains and inconveniences.

Yet, when something tragic happens, we can't help but ask, "Why me? Why am I suffering? God, why are You doing this to me?"

Instead of dismissing these questions for their selfish focus, I'd like to try to offer some possible answers. I've thought of twelve of these. See if you can think of more.

# Chapter Twenty-three: Why Me, Lord?

*"My God, my God, why have you forsaken me?"*
— Jesus, Matthew 27:46, Psalm 22:1

*"Dear friends, do not be surprised at the painful trial you are suffering, as though something strange were happening to you. But rejoice that you participate in the sufferings of Christ…"*

—Peter, 1 Peter 4:12

As a former pastor and now as a missionary strategist and life coach, I have walked alongside hundreds of people who have dealt with suffering at many levels and in many forms. Yet rarely do I encounter anyone who has stopped to analyze *why* they suffer. They may complain to anyone who will listen and pull out the "why me?" question, but most often they remain oblivious to the real and varied reasons why people suffer. I believe asking "why?" can actually help us process and discover the deeper issues that can help us long term. So let's take a look at some of the common reasons that we can come up with in answering the "why" question. I've listed twelve. You might be able to come up with a couple more.

**TWELVE REASONS I MIGHT SUFFER:**
**1. "I DESERVE IT."**

I'm suffering as a natural consequence of my own sin or stupidity. If I steal and I have to suffer in prison, I deserve it. God is then punishing me for my sin. If I trip over my shoes and split my head open, I'm suffering because of my own clumsiness, and I receive the corresponding pain that goes with it.

## 2. "I'M BEING TAUGHT A LESSON."

Much like a parent disciplining a child, I'm being corrected and given direction for future benefit. Therefore, I'm suffering the pain of the consequences that will set me straight for future decisions.

## 3. "I'M BEING PROTECTED FROM HARM."

I'm suffering now on a small scale so that I won't have to suffer much worse consequences later. I might suffer the pain of shots and treatments for the prevention of a disease that is much worse.

## 4. "I'M BEING TESTED."

God (or someone else) could be testing my faith to help me become stronger and grow. In the end, this is to see if I can handle a greater assignment, and the quicker I pass my test, the quicker I reach a higher and better place of usefulness.

## 5. "THEY DID IT TO ME."

Here, I am a victim. I've been abused, or I am the victim of a crime. I might be suffering because of my race or my gender. Perhaps I am being persecuted for my faith, or I have been unjustly accused, or I'm suffering from someone else's evil.

This reason for suffering can come in many different forms. Whether the dog ate my homework, or a drunk driver hit my child, or someone blasts me for my faith, the blame is squarely on the shoulders of others. Often I can feel powerless, fearful, and angry under these conditions.

## 6. "I AM BEING ISOLATED."

Perhaps we feel abandoned. When people are not present in our world and we feel isolated, we often wonder why no one comes to befriend us or be with us. Perhaps this feeling comes because of a relational breakdown or loss or even the death of someone close. If we don't feel God's presence, we can believe that He has abandoned us as well.

### 7. "THE DEVIL DID IT TO ME."

I'm suffering because Satan is after me. Or in the words of Flip Wilson, "The devil made me do it!" Whether I'm feeling attacked or whether I have sinned, the devil gets the credit for my suffering.

### 8. "I'VE BEEN PHYSICALLY WOUNDED."

I'm suffering because I'm sick, or I've been injured, or I have a disease, and I'm in physical pain. Whether someone else is responsible, or no one seems responsible, the fact remains that I am physically hurting.

### 9. "IT'S THE ECONOMY, STUPID!"

I may have lost my job or am hurting financially. Perhaps I feel that the economy has done me in or that the politicians are writing laws that are making my life difficult. At the core, I feel hit hard in the wallet.

### 10. "I'M FEELING FOR YOU."

I am joining in your pain to encourage and help you. Though I am a bystander, I suffer because I am in close proximity to one who is suffering. Like those who come to the scene of an accident to help the victims, I feel the pain as I try to be there for you in your pain.

### 11. "I'M BLOCKING FOR YOU."

I am suffering so that you don't have to. I'm your substitute, taking the blows, the consequences, or the punishment that is coming your way so you don't have to endure it. Jesus' death on the cross is a prime example of this. He blocked for us by paying the penalty for our sins.

And this leads us to the last reason.

### 12. "I'M SUFFERING, AND I DON'T KNOW WHY."

I've checked it out, and my suffering is a mystery to me. I see no answers. I see no reasons for my suffering. I can't figure this out. Associated with this reason is the realization that I may never receive a satisfactory answer in this life, and God may never tell me why.

**SOME ANALYSIS OF THESE REASONS:**

Whatever painful experience you are enduring right now probably falls into one of the twelve categories above. Take a minute and see if one of these categories describes why you are experiencing your pain.

As I look at these reasons, I realize that we have a tendency to assume that we suffer because of reason #12—that we don't know why. I see many who suffer who can't see the obvious. I know men who have smoked two packs of cigarettes a day for decades who are shaking their fist to heaven complaining, "Why God, did you give me lung cancer?" I've seen women who were controlling and manipulating, who sabotaged nearly every relationship they ever had, who cried out, "God, why are you letting him leave me?" Sometimes the truth hurts. And sometimes the reasons for our pain point right back to us, and we don't like it one bit.

It's like the story I heard of a two-year-old boy named Luke. One day, his dad read a bedtime story to him. The dad asked, "Luke, who made the trees?"

"Luke did!" the boy exclaimed.

"No, Luke," the father corrected. "God made the trees. Who made the mountains, Luke?"

Laughing, Luke blurted, "Luke did!"

By now, Luke is thinking this is really funny, but the dad was not going to stop trying to make his point. So he sets Luke straight again by saying, "No, God made those mountains. Who made the stars, Luke?"

"Luke did!"

"No, no, Luke, God made the stars."

Realizing he wasn't going to win this one, the dad gave up and went to bed. The next morning at breakfast, Luke spilled his milk. The dad came in and asked, "Luke, who spilled the milk?"

"God did!"

Isn't that a classic response—not just of a two-year-old boy, but of many of us who claim to be much more advanced and sophisticated than a two-year-old? If anything good happens in my life, I did it. If anything bad happens in my life, it's God's fault.

As we look at these reasons, I think it helps to bring our pains into better focus. If we suffer because of reasons #1-4, then we can just accept our responsibility for the suffering and accept the fact that growth can come from the suffering. If we suffer because of reasons #5-9, then we can feel that it's not our fault and blame it on someone or something else. Often the biggest challenge to this kind of suffering comes when we deal with the toxicity of bitterness and attempt to forgive the offender so that we can move on with our life. If we suffer because of reasons #10-11, we can feel heroic because we're helping someone. But if we suffer because of the mystery reason, reason #12, not knowing why we suffer, it creates a scenario where we wrestle with God and anyone close to us as we struggle to figure it out. Later in the book, we'll hear from a guy who wrote the definitive book on this mysterious kind of suffering.

For now, let's go back to the "Why me, Lord?" question from the beginning of this chapter. Maybe we should ask, "Why *not* me, Lord?" For some of us, when we see others who have suffered in much greater proportions than us, we wonder why we've gotten off easier than them. Perhaps you were the lone survivor of a car accident. Or a friend or family member got cancer, and you haven't done anything different than they did. I've heard several survivors ask, "Why wasn't it me instead of them?" On either side of the "why" questions, whether it's "why me?" or "why not me?" we discover that about the only way to find an answer is to look up. We're not going to find the answers for all of our whys looking for earthly answers.

Did you know that to some degree, even Jesus grappled with the mystery of suffering when he cried from the cross, "My God, my God, why have you forsaken me?" Perhaps he was quoting the first line to Psalm 22 so that His followers would remember the prophecy. Even so, I believe He truly felt those words in that moment. Earlier in the evening of his last night before being crucified the following day, Jesus prayed, asking God to "let this cup pass." But God didn't let it pass. Jesus' prayer went unanswered. At least unanswered from an earthly perspective of getting what we ask for. Have you ever stopped to ponder that Jesus prayed a prayer that went "unanswered." Why would God let Jesus down? And if God would let Jesus down, will he let us down?

I believe these questions would be good to wrestle with in the next chapter. Before we go, let me put on my boots and grab my cowboy hat. I want to introduce you to a friend who can help us continue this conversation about prayer.

# Chapter Twenty-four: Unanswered Prayer...

"Sometimes I thank God for unanswered prayers..."[1]

—Garth Brooks

"God, if I ever give You a request and You have more to give me than I am asking, cancel my request!"[2]

—Henry Blackaby's prayer in *Experiencing God*

"Never think that God's delays are God's denials. Hold on; Hold fast; Hold out. Patience is genius."[3]

—Georges-Louis Leclerc Buffon, 1707-1788
French Naturalist

If you are a country music fan, you probably know that Garth Brooks wrote a song titled *Unanswered Prayer*. The song is about an incident where he and his wife bumped into one of his old high school flames. At one time Garth had prayed that this old girlfriend would be "the one." And in looking at the two women, he realized how God had done a good thing when He didn't give him what he asked God to give him.

Like Garth, if we examine our prayer requests and the results of our prayers in hindsight, I think we might be inclined to join him in crooning a song of thanksgiving, too. Sometimes God graciously spares us of our own misguided desires.

As parents we can understand this. Sometimes our children beg us for things that would hurt them. I've seen kids scream and holler for a butcher knife, and the parent says, "No." It doesn't matter how much the little boogers bawl. A good parent is not going to budge.

My mom tells me that when I was two or three years old, I gained access to my dad's shaving cream and razor and shaved myself well enough to take a little trip to the emergency room. I got what I wanted and then some.

If God is any good at all at parenting us, wouldn't He need to periodically withhold from us what we wanted—especially if what we pleaded for might harm us? Wouldn't a loving and protecting Father say "no" to us sometimes?

Besides that, I think the notion that God doesn't always answer prayer is misunderstood, because we haven't really thought about how God might answer our prayers. Sometimes, what we deem "unanswered" has been "answered" but just not in the way we wanted.

I think the best help I've found for distinguishing this comes from Bill Hybels' classic book, *Too Busy Not to Pray*. In one of the chapters, Hybels highlights several ways to see how God answers prayer.[4]

## FOUR ANSWERS TO PRAYER:

### 1. IF THE REQUEST IS WRONG, GOD SAYS, "NO."

Like a good parent, sometimes God's answer is a simple "no." We may not like it. We may throw a temper tantrum. We may cry our little hearts out, but the answer is "no."

Jesus' early disciples sometimes did this. In Mark 10:35-45, James and John asked if they could sit on Jesus' right and left in heaven. It was a wrong request. And Jesus more than said "no." He said they didn't know what they were asking.

### 2. IF THE TIMING IS WRONG, GOD SAYS, "SLOW."

The answer is simply a matter of waiting. God didn't say "no," but "not yet." This answer to prayer will be revealed in time.

### 3. IF YOU ARE WRONG, GOD SAYS, "GROW."

Sometimes, we don't have the right character qualities to handle what we're asking God to do for us. Or we have flaws that hinder our request.

**4. IF THE REQUEST IS RIGHT, THE TIMING IS RIGHT, AND YOU ARE RIGHT, GOD SAYS, "GO!"**

This is where we get the green light—the "yes" answer. And this is what most of us think about when we imagine God answering our prayers.

Now, the fact that there are at least three answers that aren't an automatic "yes" may discourage us, but it shouldn't. In each answer, God is graciously looking out for us.

I think many of us are like the football coach who hated the passing game. When asked why, he'd say, "There are three things that can happen when you throw the ball. And two of them are bad!"

I can see how sometimes people unconsciously take a similarly negative attitude toward prayer. They might even be able to articulate it like the coach and say, "There are four things that can happen when we ask God for something, and three of them are bad."

They might try to stick their heads in the sand like an ostrich and deny the reality of the undesirable answers, or they might give up on prayer entirely—all because they don't know how to handle the "No," "Slow," and "Grow" answers.

I think many are tempted to walk away from prayer and don't even realize what they are about to give up in the process. I believe that giving up on prayer because you might get less than an automatic "yes" is about as smart as a coach saying, "I don't want to even play football because I can't handle passes that are incomplete or intercepted."

With regard to prayer, we don't need to back down or give up. We need to stay in the game. But before we strap on our helmets and get psyched up to withstand a rough prayer life, I want to give you a little chalk talk about why God might not give us the automatic "yes."

## REASONS FOR "NO," "SLOW," AND "GROW:"

**1. SIN...**

We sin when we deliberately go against God's wisdom and His ways. And when we deliberately go in a direction away from God, we shouldn't be surprised if God doesn't give us the answer we want. The people of Israel were taught this principle by many of their prophets. On one occasion, Isaiah, with his veins nearly popping in his neck, shouted...

*"Listen! The Lord is not too weak to save you, and he is not becoming deaf. He can hear you when you call. But there is a problem—your sins have cut you off from God. Because of your sin, he has turned away and will not listen anymore.*

*"Your hands are the hands of murderers, and your fingers are filthy with sin. Your mouth is full of lies, and your lips are tainted with corruption. No one cares about being fair and honest. Their lawsuits are based on lies. They spend their time plotting evil deeds and then doing them."*

Isaiah 59:1-4 (New Living Translation)

Sin messes up your prayer life. Incidentally, what should we do about sin? We admit it. We confess it to God.

*If we confess our sins, he is faithful and just and will forgive us of our sins and purify us of all unrighteousness.*

1 John 1:9

*If I had not confessed the sin in my heart, my Lord would not have listened.* Psalm 66:18 (New Living Translation)

Sin separates us from God, and God calls us to confess it. But sin is not the only factor in receiving "No," "Slow," and "Grow" answers. Here is another...

## 2. IGNORANCE.

We don't get a "yes" answer because we ask in ignorance. This is the Garth Brooks' reason for unanswered prayers. If God gave us what we wanted, it might actually hurt us or not be in our best interests.

In addition, if God has something better that He wants to give us, but we can't imagine it, God might give us something other than a "yes." Henry Blackaby helps us in *Experiencing God*. Henry's prayer at the beginning of this chapter highlights the fact that God may know something we don't know. And since that is absolutely true, why not pray with that thought in mind? Why not pray that if we are ignorant, and God has more for us than we are asking, that God automatically cancel our request?

A prayer like this puts us in a "no-lose" position, offering us a peace of mind that many find so elusive. Henry's prayer also leaves room for God to work while we live with a grateful heart—knowing that whatever God's answer, it will be the best one for us.

With that liberating thought revealed, let's flip the coin. Sometimes God gives us what we ignorantly desire. He actually allows us to have what we want and then lets us live with that reality—even if it's less than the best. Why would He do that?

Again, I think God might be like a good parent who realizes that we can learn from the reality of our choices. And when the price is affordable, perhaps His wise parenting allows us to experience the consequences of our desires.

Using the nation of Israel as an example again, the Jewish people had a time in their history when they were led by spiritual leaders— judges they called them. Yet, the people wanted to have a king like all the other nations around them. They begged for a king, and the prophet Samuel told them that God wasn't so hot on the idea. But eventually, God relented and granted their request. Samuel then introduced them to King Saul. He was tall and handsome. He had everything the people wanted. But in time, he turned out to be a brooding, psychotic man who did not lead well.

Some of you can relate to this. You begged for a particular spouse or a particular job or a particularly prized possession. Then, when you got what you wanted, your "answer" turned into a nightmare. Someone went nuts, the job went south, or the prize lost its luster.

Sometimes we just don't know what we're asking God to give us. So, if God in His sovereignty and goodness chooses not to give us an answer, we may later realize that the "non-answer" was the best thing that could have happened to us. And we just might want to join Garth in singing God's praises for "unanswered" prayers.

### 3. TIMING.

Sometimes the timing is not right. And this fits in the category of God's "slow" response. In the Bible, some of the greatest men and women of faith had to wait years for God's answer to their prayers. We observed many of them in the Hall of Fame, so I won't repeat their stories here. Their examples just underscore how most of our heroes of the faith had to wait on God. So timing issues are a common reason for what seems like unanswered prayer.

### 4. HIGHER PURPOSES.

When God wants to use us for a higher purpose, He might give us an undesirable answer. The apostle Paul was a good example of this. As we've noted before, he was one of the greatest Christians who ever lived. Yet at that point in his life, when he begged God to take away his "thorn in the flesh," God didn't do it. Later, Paul rejoiced in what God did through his unanswered prayer by making His power evident in Paul's weakness.

### 5. WE DON'T KNOW.

This reason for the "No," "Slow," and "Grow" comes when God alone knows the answer. Sometimes God remains silent, and we can't understand it. I will say more about this in the next chapter, but for now I want to take a minute to reflect a little.

As I reviewed this material for the second edition, I've had a little more time to reflect on God's answers to some of my big, life-altering prayers. Just this morning I was pondering the way God answered my prayer by the lake at Willow Creek. When I prayed that God would bring a church like that to Kansas City, I believed to the core of my being that the answer was clear—"Yes, you will get to see this, but it will require more sacrifice than you can imagine." During that prayer time, I even felt that God gave me a number. I believed He wanted to bring 10,000 people together in 10 years.

Now that it has been almost twenty years since that defining moment, how do I interpret God's answer? For starters, I did not pastor a church that grew to 10,000 in 10 years. So did I really hear from God? Well, *I* didn't get to lead a church that grew like that, but a friend of mine did. At the time I was praying by the lake at Willow Creek, my friend, Adam Hamilton, was starting the United Methodist Church of the Resurrection—in a funeral home! Ten years later they had over 10,000 people attend Easter services and have had scores of people come to Christ. In addition, as I scan the church landscape in our region, I see at least four other churches that God has raised up with a great heart to reach out to the unchurched like what I was so inspired about that first time I walked on the grounds of Willow Creek. God is true to His word. He answered my prayer beyond what I asked for, but it wasn't easy for me to see.

Part of the sacrifice that I didn't understand for many years was my assumption that I was supposed to be the leader of the parade. But God never promised me that. He just promised that I would get to see it happen. While I can't deny the pain and the anguish of getting to this realization, I have reached a place of gratitude for God's denial of me fulfilling a role that I so desperately wanted.

As I write to you today, my crisis of belief doesn't really bother me anymore. Because of the many inroads we've made with different people groups in Guatemala, and because of the many lessons learned about creating simple churches that don't require pastoral CEO's to lead, I believe that God has had a higher purpose for me. Maybe I'm a slow learner, but I'm discovering ways to reach cowboys and Kekchi Indians that I believe could transform the way we reproduce disciples and churches here in the U.S. One day I hope to write about that.

But for now, I want to reemphasize the point that God really does answer our prayers. I can see now more than ever how God has been scripting my life story into something that is beyond what I could have ever dreamed. I think I'm really okay with God putting me in a place where I may never see the full results of my labors on this side of the pearly gates. I think I really am okay with the mystery of not having the whole picture.

And that leads me back to where we ended the last chapter. We have now come back around to an acknowledgement of the mystery factor in the realm of suffering. In that last chapter, I promised you that we'd tackle it head on. Now let's do it.

To get the perspective we need, I want to take you to a dinner theater. There we will meet up with the guy who some might say "wrote the book" on suffering. I've got to warn you. If you've got a queasy stomach, be wary of eating too much while you watch the play. There are a few scenes that are not too appetizing. Are you ready? Good. Let's go.

# Chapter Twenty-five: The Guy Who Wrote the Book on Suffering...

*In the land of Uz there lived a man whose name was Job. This man was blameless and upright; he feared God and shunned evil.* Job 1:1

*"In this life, good people are often treated as though they were wicked, and wicked people are often treated as though they were good."*
—Solomon, Ecclesiastes 8:14 (New Living Translation)

No treatment on suffering would be complete without a look at the guy in the Bible who you might say could have written the definitive book on suffering. His name? Job. He's the star of the show we're about to watch, and his story is a fascinating one. Now, to be accurate, the biblical book that bears his name may not have been written *by* him. But it was certainly written *about* him. Job was a wealthy guy who seemed to have it all. He was one of the richest men of his day. He had a great lifestyle, a wonderful family, and it seemed that the more he served God, the more God blessed him.

John Ortberg, when he was a teaching pastor at Willow Creek Community Church, preached an in-depth message from the book of Job to the mid-week crowd at Willow. His message was titled "Where is God When It Hurts?"[1] And in it, Ortberg did a masterful job at boiling down the book of Job. He began by noting that the book of Job is like a play done on two stages for the audience.

That imagery really helped me better understand this challenging book. As a way of getting you immersed in this material, I want to take Ortberg's theatrical metaphor and run with it a little further than he did. I want to use it as a way to retell the story of Job. By doing so, I hope to give you a stronger grip on the big ideas in this book, and it may prompt you to reread the book of Job and see if what I've done here is faithful to the story.

Ortberg showed us that in Job's book, it's as if there is an upper stage and a lower stage. On the upper stage, God has a conversation with Satan, an adversarial character who wants to take Job down. The audience is aware of that dialogue. Then, also in full view of the audience, action takes place on the lower stage. And this is where Job plays out his life before us. Note that Job has no idea what is being said or done on the upper stage. All he knows is what happens on the lower stage. But we, as a part of the audience, have full knowledge of what is said and done on both the upper and lower stages.

Now, as the play begins, God asks Satan if he's noticed His star follower—Job. He says, "Now there's a fine, upright guy who worships Me and resists evil."

Satan replies, "Yeah, but he's only that way because You're his Sugar Daddy! Every time he does something good, You bless him. But if You were to stop doing that and let him lose all he has, I'll bet he'd change his tune and even curse You to Your face!"

"Alright then," God says. "Let's see what happens. You can take everything he's got, but don't lay a finger on him. He's My guy."

At this point, the lights fade on the upper stage as they come up on the lower stage. On that lower stage we see Job standing before a servant. The servant, in a distressing tone of voice says, "They came out of nowhere! Some bandits took the oxen and donkeys! Then, they ran their swords through everyone they saw! I was the only one who managed to escape."

While that servant is speaking, another one crawls in gasping and breathless. "I was out with the sheep, and without warning, a bolt of lightening struck! It started a fire that burned up all the sheep, and all the other sheepherders. I am the only one that survived."

While he is speaking, another messenger comes sprinting in and blurts, "Bad news boss. Some camel rustlers came in on us in three raids and took all of your camels. What's worse, they killed everybody. I was the only one who got away."

While this servant is still speaking, another one barges in, and this one looks like he's seen a ghost. He says, "Master, I was near your son's house where your sons and daughters were enjoying a meal together. Suddenly, a tornado-like wind swept in from the desert and the roof fell in on them. I am the only one who survived."

At all this, Job rips his shirt, falls to his knees, and cries, "Naked I came into this world, and naked I will leave it. The Lord gives, and the Lord takes away. Blessed be the name of the Lord."

As the lights slowly fade on Job and come back up on the upper stage, the narrator says, "In all this, Job did not sin."

And God says to Satan, "What do you think now about my man Job? He's still showing his true character."

"Sure, he's staying true to You," Satan replies. "But nothing's happened to *him*. I guarantee if You strike his health and his body, he'll turn on You."

"Alright," God says. "Let's take it to the next level. You can take his health. But you must not take his life."

Again, the lights fade on the upper stage, and we see Job sitting in a garbage dump, using a piece of broken pottery to scrape off the ooze from the boils that now cover his body. In walks Mrs. Job. She's grieving the loss of her children. She's distraught. And in a fit of anger, she cries toward Job, "Why don't you just curse God and die?!"

"Foolish woman," Job replies, "shall we accept good from God and not trouble?"

As the lights fade on this scene, the narrator says, "And Job did not sin in what he *said*." The implication is that Job might be *thinking* a lot more than he's *saying*. The curtain is rising for the next act, so let's watch.

The scene begins with three men talking as they walk down the road. One of them says, "I hope what we heard about Job proves to be worse than it really is."

Another agrees, "Yeah, and I hope that we can cheer him up. He's got to be shaken by the loss of his children."

The third one looks into the distance. "Hey guys. We're getting close. Do you think that's him?"

"It can't be. That guy looks like a tramp. And Job is such a snappy dresser."

"I don't know; I think it's him."

"That man looks like his skin is rotting."

They all come to the stark realization at the same time. "It's him!" they exclaim in horror.

Job comes onto the stage limping and dragging his back foot. His face is scarred, and he reeks of dead flesh. His friends fall to the ground weeping. And after a time, they sit on the floor with Job, not saying a word.

The narrator says, "They sat on the ground with Job for seven days and seven nights. No one said a word to him, because they saw how much he was suffering. After the seventh day, Job spoke."

"May the day I was born be cursed! May the night when they passed out cigars saying, 'It's a boy!' be cursed as well. May those who curse days curse that day. Why didn't I just die at birth? My worst nightmares have come to pass. I'm in constant turmoil, and I can't even get a good night's sleep."

As the lights fade on an angry Job, his friends sit with him in silence. After a moment of darkness, Act Three begins. The narrator says, "After a week of listening to Job's complaining, his friends finally begin to speak."

Let's listen in on some sound bites from these speeches and Job's responses.

### ELIPHAZ:

"Job, up until now, you've been a model citizen. You've been an encouragement to all who come in contact with you. And your faith in God has been stellar. But now I have a question. Who, being innocent, was ever destroyed? As I have observed, he who plows evil and sows trouble will reap it.

"God has given me a word for you. It came in a dream. In it, God said, 'Can a mortal be more righteous than Me? Can a man be more pure than his Maker?'

"Job, God has corrected you. And blessed be the man whom God corrects! Do not despise His discipline. He wounds you, but He also can heal you. If you follow God's course of discipline, you can be restored. Hear my words and apply them to yourself."

**JOB:**

"If I could weigh my anguish right now, it would weigh more than all the sand on the seashore. I know I spoke impulsively. But I hurt!

"I agree that it appears that God is letting me have it. At this point, my prayers are, 'God, go ahead and finish me off! I'm done!'

"Right now, I don't have the power to do anything. And a despairing man should at least have his friends. But my friends are as undependable as the waters that flow in a dry gulch. They look promising in times of rain, but they are nowhere to be found when the weather gets dry and times are hard. You guys are proving to be no help. God, if I have sinned, what have I done to You? Why have You made me a target?"

**BILDAD:**

"How long are you going to carry on? You're blowing a bunch of hot air. Does God pervert justice? When your children sinned against Him, He gave them over to their sin, and they paid for it. Job, it's simple. Sin has consequences. But if you ask God to forgive you of your sin, He will restore you.

"Ask any of the old-timers who have been around longer than both of us, and I think they will tell you that I'm right. Surely God does not reject a blameless man or serve as an accomplice to an evil man. Repent, and God will bring joy and laughter back into your life."

**JOB:**

"I know that much of what you say is true, but how can a mere mortal be righteous before God? His wisdom and power is so much bigger and more vast than anything we can comprehend.

"Although I am blameless, I don't care anymore. I just want to be put out of my misery and have God take my life. I see how God destroys both the upright and the wicked.

"Let's face it, I have a huge complaint I want to present to God. I feel like I've been judged and pronounced guilty without a trial. I wish I could take God to court and have an attorney to defend my case. I wish I could speak up for myself. But as it is, I can't.

"God, it feels like You have abandoned me! It seems You bring new witnesses against me and that Your anger against me is escalating. Why did You even let me live? Turn your back on me, and let me die in peace."

## ZOPHAR:

"I can't sit over here and let you get away with what you're saying. Somebody needs to correct your faulty thinking before you say another word. You say to God that you are pure and faultless in His sight. That makes me want to gag! I wish God would speak the truth right now and put you in your place. You've lost your mind.

"God has already forgotten some of your sin, so you ought to be grateful that it's not worse. Surely God can spot a deceitful man a mile away, and He takes notes on those who do evil. You can't fake God out. You can't prove that you are something you're not any more than a person without a brain can show that he is wise. It's about as absurd as thinking a donkey can give birth to a human baby. It's impossible.

"Job, face up to your sin. If you put it away and you devote your heart to Him, then you can lift up your face without shame and live with a great hope, and your darkness will be turned into light."

## JOB:

"Well now. The people have spoken. It looks like wisdom is going to die with you, because you appear to know it all. Guys, I'm not stupid! I have a brain, and I'm not beneath you in your knowledge. What you say about God being a good Creator and One who hates evil is nothing new to me. What I keep coming back to is the fact that I've not done anything out of the ordinary to deserve this. Yet, I have become a laughingstock to my friends. All the influential people in town have written me off. But God knows the truth. And He can set the record straight.

"I know I'm contradicting myself when I say that I want to die. But I want to be faithful to God. I do want to believe in Him. And though He slays me, I will still put my hope in Him.

"I wish I knew how long I'd have to endure this. If I knew that, I think I could make it. I think I could hang on with less mental turmoil. How I long for the day when this is over."

## LONG SPEECHES KEEP COMING...

Let's take a break in the action here. As you can see, the pattern is set. Job's friends keep saying, "Job, you must have sinned big time here to have all this bad stuff happen to you. Why don't you just repent and admit it to God so that He can restore you?"

And Job keeps saying something like, "Guys, I haven't done anything wrong. I have been faithful to God. I would gladly repent, but I don't have anything to repent of at the moment."

Job does contradict himself in his long statements of defense. At times he wants God to just put him out of his misery so he can die. At other times he defends himself and wants to be vindicated. And at other times he expresses his desire to live for God no matter what the cost and no matter what the circumstances. Like many who suffer, Job's pain causes him to be inconsistent. And in Job's case, it creates further opportunities for his friends to come back with their lectures to tell Job what he should do. After Job's friends each had a couple of shots at him, and after Job responded to each one, Elihu, a young whippersnapper who has listened to all of them butts in and says...

## ELIHU:

"I have had it with all this talk! I know I am younger than all of you, and for that reason I've held off saying anything. But no more. I must speak. I am ashamed of all three of you! You haven't refuted Job or answered his arguments. And Job, I cannot believe you would continue to try to defend yourself, saying you haven't done anything wrong."

## THE DOCTRINE OF RETRIBUTION

Even though Elihu claims to have something different to say that should repudiate Job, when you read his speech, it sounds similar to what the others said. And, it appears to be the longest sermon of any of them.

John Ortberg says that the essence of the sermons of Job's friends can be summed up in one phrase. It's the *doctrine of retribution*. It's the belief system that states that we get what we deserve. If something good happens to me, it means I did something good and God is rewarding me for it. If something bad happens to me, it means I have sinned and I must be paying for that.

Therefore, if something *really* bad happens to me, I must have done something *really* bad for me to deserve it. In this view, there is always a reason for what happens. You just have to look hard sometimes to find it.

So Job's friends hound him with accusatory questions, trying to help him remember the terrible things he did while he was living the good life. Perhaps he neglected to do something or repressed a hidden sin. And now these hidden things are the reasons that God would punish him. If Job could figure it out and repent of it, they are confident that God would give him his life back, and all could sing a merry tune.

## THE END OF THE STORY...

As the lights fade on all those still offering speeches on the lower stages, the lights come up again on the upper stage as the narrator says, "Then the LORD answered Job out of the storm..." In a whirlwind that moves from the upper stage to the lower stage, we hear God speak from the middle of that storm. Job finally gets his wish, and God speaks to him. Let's listen.

## GOD:

"Who is this that obscures the truth of My words? Who speaks without knowledge? Brace yourself and answer Me. Where were you when I laid the foundation of the earth? Who was it that figured out how big it should be? Who here can run the universe? Have you ever given orders to the sun or shown the dawn its place? Tell Me about this creation. Surely you were born before it was all put together. Please tell Me these things from your vast knowledge. Can you control the world of nature? Do you know when the mountain goats give birth? Who lets the wild donkey run free? Did you have anything to do with the creation of the ostrich? She's a silly creature but one endowed with speed and

162

amazing abilities. What about the horse? Do you make him leap on strong hind legs and charge fearless into battle? Does the hawk fly because of your wisdom? Does the eagle soar on your command? Will the one who contends with the Almighty speak up now and correct Him?"

**JOB:**

"I am unworthy. How can I reply to You? I should keep my lips zipped up. I spoke once, but now I have no answer."

**GOD:**

"Brace yourself and take this like a man. I have further questions for you. Would you discredit my justice? Would you condemn Me to justify yourself? Do you have an arm like Mine and a voice that thunders like this? If so, unleash your wrath. Zap those who you think deserve it.

"I'm still the Creator here. Look at the hippopotamus. I had my 'A' game going when I created him. Can you control him? Or what about the alligator? Can you wrestle him down and turn him into a docile pet like Tweety Bird?"

**JOB:**

"I know that You can do all things. You asked, 'Who is it that obscures My words?' Well, it was me. I spoke about things I did not understand. I wanted to take You to court and hear from You. Now that I have seen You, I feel so small. I need to repent of my arrogance."

**NARRATOR:**

"After the Lord and Job had these words with each other, the Lord spoke to Eliphaz, saying..."

**GOD:**

"I am angry with you and your two friends, because you have not spoken for Me. In fact, what you said was wrong, and Job was right. Make a sacrifice to atone for your sins—seven bulls and seven rams should do it. Then go and have My servant Job pray for you. Then I won't hold you responsible for your foolishness."

**NARRATOR:**

"The three friends did what God asked of them, and Job prayed for his friends. After Job prayed, the Lord restored Job and made him prosperous again and gave him twice as much as he had before. The Lord blessed the latter part of Job's life more than the first. He gave him seven sons and three daughters, and his daughters were certifiable knockouts. Job lived to a ripe old age, getting to enjoy his children, grandchildren, great grandchildren, and even a few great, great grandchildren."

## LESSONS LEARNED FROM JOB...

As the curtain falls for the last time on the book of Job, what are the lessons we can take with us? For one, we learn that the doctrine of retribution is dead wrong. While God wants to reward us for being faithful to Him, He has chosen not to make it a linear, one-for-one correlation. Sometimes good doesn't seem to get rewarded, and bad doesn't seem to get punished. And through it all, God doesn't seem to feel the least bit obligated to tell us why.

Even when God "answered" Job, how did He answer? With questions! Job wanted to know why God would let him suffer so. Did he get an answer? Nope. God never gave him a direct answer. God just came back with a question like, "Who's qualified here to run the universe?" Clearly, a part of the lesson learned from this story is that God is the Creator, and we're not. And God doesn't always tell us *why* something happens.

After God's response, Job didn't come back to any of his previous questions. He didn't say, "God, You've made Your point about Who is in charge here quite well. But You haven't answered my question about why *I* have to suffer." No, Job was able to let it go in that moment and live without the answers.

Blake Elliott, a good friend of mine who has suffered through the lingering effects of a near fatal car crash over 30 years ago, told me that he believes that this reality just might be true for us when we get to heaven. Many of us will be concerned with questions we want to ask God when we pass through those pearly gates. But when we actually see our Savior face to face, Blake wonders if we'll naturally respond like Job and see that it just does not matter. I think he's right.

One person who has lived through a Job-like nightmare is Dr. Helen Roseveare. In her book, *Give Me This Mountain*, she talks about her life as a missionary doctor in the Belgian Congo.[2] In August of 1964, a bloody civil war broke out. In about five months, 27 missionaries were killed, more than 200 Roman Catholic priests and nuns were murdered, and nearly a quarter of a million innocent African civilians were butchered.

At the beginning of the hostilities, rebel soldiers crashed through Helen's door, beat her, and violated her. Bloodied and hurt, with teeth missing from being kicked in the mouth, Helen experienced an unusual peace in her pain. During the worst of her suffering, Helen explained how God spoke to her. God said, "Can you thank Me for trusting you with this, even if I never tell you why?"

Helen tells audiences, "You and I think of us trusting Him. But the thought that He wants to trust us—that was something very new to my thinking."[3]

Helen says that she realized that God somehow trusted her with something that most could not have handled. And that realization helped her go on from that horrible day.

I believe Job experienced a similar thing. God wasn't going to give him answers to his "Why?" questions. God just trusted Job with something that not everyone could have handled. And once he had that final encounter with God, it changed his focus.

Now, beyond the reactions of God and Job, I believe we can extrapolate some things from Job's story that Job couldn't get in the middle of his crisis. Remember, we got to see the scene from the upper stage. While Job was asking, "Why?" we knew the answer. We knew that God wanted to see if one of His best and most dedicated worshippers would stay true to Him even while enduring immense amounts of suffering.

In Ortberg's message, he noted several tests taking place, and these tests come from the players on the two stages. On the lower stage, God is put to the test by Job and his friends. They have the least knowledge of what is really happening, but they wrestle with what God is doing or not doing.

On the upper stage, Job is getting tested. Satan played a role like a prosecuting attorney, and God served as Job's defender. Think about that one for a minute. Even when Job wanted to take God to court for the way he was treated, God had already spoken on his behalf on the upper stage. Still, Job never had the privilege of knowing that. He had to live in the dark, painful, and uncertain reality that nearly drove him crazy.

In the end, we saw how Job's friends were tested by God and how they flunked their test. They had a chance to comfort and encourage Job. And though they started well when they sat with Job for the first seven days, they failed when they began to speak.

Ortberg says that today, the sons and daughters of Job have the same opportunity to prove Satan wrong. We can live our lives in such a way as to demonstrate that some people really can love God and trust God for no apparent payback at all.

From Job we understand that some suffering comes to faithful God-followers that will make no sense. Some will suffer disproportionately to others, and we will not be given an answer that satisfies on this lower stage where we live.

Yet, Job also gives us a glimpse behind the curtain to the upper stage, where we can see that God does not overlook anything. In the end, He *will* come through for those on the lower stage. Not one person will fall through the cracks of heaven and get lost in the shuffle. Not one.

Now, those of us bearing our suffering clause in this life can know several things.

### 1. OUR LIVES REALLY DO COUNT.

We really can make a difference in eternity. What we do with our lives really matters. We will not realize the full extent of it now, but one day we will.

### 2. BE WARY OF THE DOCTRINE OF RETRIBUTION.

Jesus too had to fight this destructive doctrine. In Luke 13, we're told that Jesus was in the middle of a teaching session when someone in the crowd asked him to comment on the headlines of that day. Two tragedies had taken place. One had to do with a group of worshippers at a temple in Galilee. Pilate (who washed his hands of Jesus' blood at Jesus' crucifixion) ordered some worshippers there to be killed, and their blood mixed with the blood from the sacrifices on the altar. Pilate's act was a horrible, despicable deed perpetrated on innocent people. And he did it to put terror in the hearts of those who might oppose him.

The other incident Jesus mentioned was the collapse of a large tower, which had fallen and killed 18 unsuspecting people. Some wondered if these people had it coming to them. "Do you think these people were more sinful than others around them?" Jesus asked with a rising level of agitation in his voice. When no one answered, Jesus cried out...

*"I tell you, no! But unless you repent, you too will all perish."* Luke 13:5

Jesus would say, "These people were no worse than you." They didn't deserve this more than anyone else. And then Jesus went further to say that even so, it should serve as a wake-up call to all—that our lives are short and that we should repent of our sins before it's too late.

Do you think the same kind of thing might appear in the headlines today? Do you think the doctrine of retribution is still wreaking havoc more than 2000 years after Jesus' earthly ministry? You better believe it.

Friends and preachers and ministries all around us continue to espouse some version of this doctrine of retribution. A good example of this came after September 11th, when many proclaimed that the real cause for the tragedy was not so much the sin of the perpetrators, but the sin of our nation. And many of these so-called prophets seemed to know precisely which of our many sins it was that caused God to judge us. To those who lost loved ones, who like Job would say, "I don't think my loved one sinned any more than the next guy to deserve this," others piped in, "But surely your loved one must have done something."

Undoubtedly, this doctrine is still being fed to us now, well into the twenty-first century. Please, don't swallow it. And for God's sake, don't serve it to those who in Job-like proportions mysteriously suffer for things we can't explain. Don't pile on to those who suffer by dishing out this pious-sounding but half-baked heresy. Just because it may be proclaimed by popular preachers or evangelists should not sway us into falling for this devastating philosophy.

With that said, let me warn you. Some of you, during a time of suffering, will be hit by the doctrine of retribution. Armchair theologians will come to you to explain your pain in some version of this belief system. Remember, you aren't the first to endure it. Job and the descendants of Job have had to weather this injustice before you, and you can too. Realize that this is part of your suffering clause. Hold on to your faith. Don't give up on your loving Creator. Never forget that He is fully capable of fighting your battles and will take up your case—serving as your leading defender in the trials of your life.

Much more could be said on this subject, but I think the theater folks would like us to move on so they can clean up. I'd like to continue our conversation by looking at the genuine hope that people like Job can have even in the middle of their most difficult days. If you come with me to the next chapter, I want to show you that there is a hope available to you in this world that has your name on it. No, it's not some elaborate time-share deal. It's something very real and very personal. Let's take a look at it.

# Chapter Twenty-six: Hope with Your Name on it...

"Once you choose hope, anything is possible."[1]

—Christopher Reeve

"Hope is patience with the lamp lit."[2]

—Tertullian

*"I pray also that the eyes of your heart may be enlightened in order that you may know the hope to which he has called you, the riches of his glorious inheritance in the saints, and his incomparably great power for us who believe. That power is like the working of his mighty strength, which he exerted in Christ when he raised him from the dead and seated him at his right hand in the heavenly realms, far above all rule and authority, power and dominion, and every title that can be given, not only in the present age but also in the one to come."*

— Paul, Ephesians 1:18-21

*"We also rejoice in our sufferings, because we know that suffering produces perseverance; perseverance, character; and character, hope. And hope does not disappoint us, because God has poured out his love into our hearts by the Holy Spirit, whom he has given us."*

— Paul, Romans 5:3-5

When I read the above passages of scripture penned from our suffering clause hero, the Apostle Paul, I get goose bumps. Paul saw hope where many didn't. To him, it was clear. Everybody can have hope. In the verse above, Paul offers up a prayer for his Ephesian brothers that I believe extends to us—to "those who believe." Imagine the old veteran of many hardships, writing from another nameless prison cell, longing to put his hands on your shoulders and pray for you.

With his eyes wide open, I can see Paul looking directly into your eyes, praying this blessing on your life. "May your eyes be opened so you can see what God sees—that there is a hope with your name on it." Paul continues, "May you see that spiritual riches await you, and may you see that His power is at work right now in you. May you see that this power is the very same resurrection power that propelled Christ from the grave and put Him on His heavenly throne."

Hope with your name on it. Paul says it's real. And he says it's available to us—especially in our suffering. In the Romans 5 passage I just quoted, Paul retraces the steps of what happens when we faithfully endure suffering. Suffering produces perseverance, and that's good. Perseverance then produces character. That's certainly good. And then good character produces what? Yeah. It produces hope. Not a fake, conjured-up kind of hope, mind you, but a real hope that is deeper than anything else in this world. This hope will never disappoint us and comes guaranteed with the very presence of God, the Holy Spirit in our lives.

And because of all that, we can rejoice. We can cut loose and shout, "Hallelujah!" because we have something that can't be bought or sold or taken away from us. It's ours. And no one in this world can steal it. No person, no circumstance, no country, no government, no school, no church, no antagonist, no mom, no dad, no friend, no enemy, ABSOLUTELY NO ONE has the power to rip this hope from your life! This one is yours, and it's for keeps.

So, for the rest of our days, we can have a hope that we cling to while we live on the lower stage—knowing that great and cosmic things have happened way over our heads to guarantee that our hope will be well founded in the end. Why is it well founded? Because this hope rests on the real-life resurrection of Jesus.

When I think of this, I can't help but think about Dr. Gary Habermas, one of the leading experts on the resurrection, and one who has written several books on the subject. In Lee Strobel's book, *The Case for Christ*, Strobel interviews Dr. Habermas to talk about whether the biblical accounts of the resurrection can be trusted. For much of their meeting, Habermas focused on rational reasons for the resurrection. But at the end of the interview, the conversation turned personal. Strobel recounts the way Habermas spoke about his wife Debbie, who died a few years earlier from stomach cancer. During her last days, Habermas recalled how his students tried to cheer him up. Here's Strobel's account of what he said.

> "Do you know what was amazing? My students would call me—not just one, but several of them—and say, 'At a time like this, aren't you glad about the Resurrection?' As sober as those circumstances were, I had to smile for two reasons. First, my students were trying to cheer me up with my own teaching. And second, it worked!

> "As I would sit there, I'd picture Job, who went through all that terrible stuff and asked questions of God, but then God turned the tables and asked *him* a few questions.

> "I knew if God were to come to me, I'd ask only one question: 'Lord, why is Debbie up there in bed?' And I think God would respond by asking gently, 'Gary, did I raise my Son from the dead?'

> "I'd say, 'Come on Lord, I've written seven books on that topic! Of course he was raised from the dead. But I want to know about Debbie!'

> "I think he'd keep coming back to the same question—'Did I raise my Son from the dead?' 'Did I raise my Son from the dead?'—until I got His point: the Resurrection says that if Jesus was raised two thousand years ago, there's an answer to Debbie's death in 1995. And do you know what? It worked for me while I was sitting on the porch, and it still works today...

> "That's not some sermon," he said quietly. "I believe that with all my heart. If there's a resurrection, there's a heaven. If Jesus was raised, Debbie was raised. And I will be someday too. Then I'll see them both."[3]

Even great theologians need hope in a dark circumstance. As you read those touching and powerful words of Dr. Habermas, perhaps your thoughts were turned to someone close to you who has suffered. When I think of a theologian who suffered, I can't help but think of my friend, Tony Rengifo. Tony was a friend of my family for years. When my parents were missionaries in Peru, we got acquainted with Tony and his wife Renee. Tony grew up in the jungles of Peru, and even in that setting, it was apparent that Tony was gifted with a keen intellect. Because of the foresight of a missionary, he was given an opportunity to go to the United States to study. After gaining a couple of degrees, Tony returned to Peru to serve as a pastor, and that's where he and my dad became lifelong friends and colleagues.

After serving as a pastor, Tony felt the call to teach in a seminary and returned to the United States for further training. He loved theological education and particularly loved teaching students in Latin America. For many years he taught in a seminary in Costa Rica, and then for a short time he taught in Mexico. All along the way, he worked in churches and in various missionary endeavors outside the classroom. During one particular ministry run, he had taken an assignment to reach out to medical doctors and those in the medical community. In San José, Costa Rica, one such group quickly grew into one of the strongest churches of his denomination in that country. Because of that success, he was asked to replicate the same kind of thing in Mexico City while also leading a seminary there.

As I was nearing the completion of the first edition of this book, Tony called my Dad and said, "Don, I need your help." For about a month, Tony had been battling a mysterious ailment that was literally eating him alive—causing him to lose weight at an alarming rate. That day, one of Tony's doctor friends had diagnosed it as a rapidly advancing cancer that had to be addressed immediately. So Tony and Renee hastily packed a suitcase and flew to Kansas City where my parents arranged for Tony to see a nationally respected oncologist.

At first the prognosis seemed good. They'd caught the cancer in an early enough stage to do something about it. That first week, as I visited Tony in the hospital, I asked if he needed reading material and offered a rough draft of some of the chapters of the book. Tony was a sponge for any material like this, and he eagerly agreed for me to bring it to him. I looked forward to having visits with Tony and having him critique my work and give me his insights. A couple of days later, I brought him the manuscript and left for the airport for a weeklong engagement in California. As I left Tony's room, he looked stronger than the week before.

A week later, as I was flying home, I had a connecting flight in Denver. I called my wife from there to make sure she knew my plane was on time. She got straight to the point. "Steve, Tony is not doing well," she said. "Something happened, and he's dying. When I pick you up at the airport, we're going to need to get you to the hospital to see Tony. He's not expected to make it through the night."

As soon as I hit the ground in K.C., we hurried to the hospital. There, in ICU, Tony hung on with all he had. Each breath, while being aided by a ventilator, was like that of a man coming up from having been under water—gasping for air. In that state he couldn't talk, but he seemed aware of much of what was going on around him. Renee asked me if I would pray for Tony. I did. And as I prayed, I felt one of the most helpless feelings I've ever had in my life. I fumbled around for words to say. I think I prayed for things like love and strength and for Tony to experience the peace of God right there in that moment. It was not a prayer of great faith on my part.

I felt powerless from it all. Everything happened way too fast. Tony wasn't supposed to go down this quickly. Selfishly, I had hoped that Tony would get to read my book and we would have some deep conversations about it. But I realized I needed to let him go. Nola and I went home. The next day, we got the call. Tony died.

As we moved through the next few days with Tony's family and friends, the "hope with Tony's name on it" became very evident. Tony had invested his life in that hope. And it was comforting to see some of the fruits of his ministry. Memorial services were held in several countries where Tony had served. Hundreds of people in each place came out to testify of his impact on their lives. We remembered some of the funny things Tony said and did. And we comforted one another with our hope that one day we will get to join Tony in the place where our ultimate hopes are finally realized. And on that great day, we will get to move from the lower stage to the upper stage and see our Savior face to face.

Because of that hope, I look forward to one day getting a chance to carry on the conversation that Tony and I started but didn't get to finish. And on that day, Tony will get to tell me what he thinks of my book. And because of the lead time he's got on me, I'm sure he will have boned up on the subject to tell me of some great intellectual discovery he's made in heaven that impacts everything I tried to write about!

As bearers of this hope, we have a great privilege and a great responsibility to share it with others—especially to those who are hurting. But sharing that hope can be tricky. When we have opportunities to try to help those who suffer, what can we say? What can we do to help them? Let's look at that in our next chapter.

# Chapter Twenty-seven: Helping Those Who Hurt...

"I have found the paradox that if I love until it hurts, then there is no hurt, but only more love."[1]

—Mother Teresa

*"Praise be to the God and Father of our Lord Jesus Christ, the Father of compassion and the God of all comfort, who comforts us in all our troubles, so that we can comfort those in any trouble with the comfort we ourselves have received from God. For just as the sufferings of Christ flow over into our lives, so also through Christ our comfort overflows. If we are distressed, it is for your comfort and salvation; if we are comforted, it is for your comfort, which produces in you patient endurance of the same sufferings we suffer. And our hope for you is firm, because we know that just as you share in our sufferings, so also you share in our comfort."*

— Paul, 2 Corinthians 1:3-7

*"If you have any encouragement from being united with Christ, if any comfort from his love, if any fellowship with the Spirit, if any tenderness and compassion, then make my joy complete by being like-minded, having the same love, being one in spirit and purpose. Do nothing out of selfish ambition or vain conceit, but in humility consider others better than yourselves. Each of you should look not only to your own interests, but also to the interests of others."*

— Paul, Philippians 2:1

*"So then, those who suffer according to God's will should commit themselves to their faithful Creator and continue to do good."*

—Peter, 1 Peter 4:19

When it comes to helping those who hurt, Philip Yancey, in his book, *Where is God When It Hurts?*, says that no "one-size-fits-all" phrase exists that will help every person who suffers. In fact, when he asked those who suffer what people said to them that helped them the most, he found inconsistencies in their answers. Some fondly remembered a friend who cheerily distracted them and helped them forget their troubles, while others found that same approach insulting.

In short, Yancey found no magic cure for a person in pain. But he did find a common emotion that cut through the maze of human suffering. It is love. Yancey surmises that the reason behind this notion is that love instinctively detects what a person needs. Jean Vanier, the founder of l'Arche movement, says it well for Yancey: "Wounded people who have been broken by suffering and sickness ask for only one thing: a heart that loves and commits itself to them, a heart full of hope for them."[2]

Yancey goes on to say that the answer to the question, "How do I help those who hurt?" is exactly the same as the answer to the question, "How do I love?" In the language of 1 Corinthians 13, "I can speak in the tongues of men and of angels...but without love, I am nothing." Love cuts through human suffering like nothing else.[3]

Dr. T.B. Maston, a long-time professor of ethics at Southwestern Baptist Theological Seminary, demonstrated this. When I attended Southwestern in the mid-80's, Dr. Maston had been retired for over 20 years. Yet, even at the age of 90 years old, he was still growing and learning. Each day, when the weather permitted, he'd shuffle over to the campus library from his home located just a block from the seminary.

One day, Dr. Maston was asked to speak to a class on the nature of race relations. Dr. Maston spoke courageously for civil rights in the 50's and 60's—even before men like Dr. Martin Luther King, Jr. had gained a national audience. As Dr. Maston spoke, I was spellbound. And when the class was over, I spoke with him.

Realizing that he was tiring a bit, I asked him if I could walk him home. He obliged—I think realizing that I wanted to glean as much wisdom from him as I could. As we walked, we kept the conversation flowing, and I savored every moment we had as we ambled across the campus and down the street.

When we got to the door, he said, "If you have a minute, I'd like to introduce you to my wife and my son."

"Sure, that sounds great," I said, grateful that I'd get a few more minutes with him. We entered into the back door of his home. His wife, Essie Mae, who T.B. affectionately called "Mommie," greeted me, and then Dr. Maston walked me over to meet his son, "Tom Mac," who was sitting in a wheelchair.

Dr. Maston said, "This is Tom Mac, and he has lived contentedly for over 60 years in a wheelchair." I went over and touched his hand as I heard Tom Mac say, "aye," the one word he could vocalize.

At Tom Mac's birth, both he and Essie Mae nearly died. Due to the rigors of that traumatic birth, Tom Mac experienced an injury to his brain that caused him to have cerebral palsy and resulted in a lifelong, spastic paralysis. For over six decades, T.B. and "Mommie" had lovingly cared for their son. And this day was no different.

Dr. Maston continued, "Tom Mac has taught me so much through the years." And he went on to describe how many of the things he'd written had come from what he learned while caring for Tom Mac. As I watched them, only one word described the scene. It was "love." They loved one another and seemed to delight in being with one another.

Through the years, Dr. Maston was one of the most vocal advocates for missions and for missionaries in his denomination. He repeatedly told people who were considering a call to missions, "If you cannot love people of all colors, classes, and conditions of life, I suggest you don't go."[4]

In a similar way, if you feel called to help a hurting person, I think the same advice applies. If you can't love a person regardless of color, class, disposition, or condition in life, you won't do well in helping people who are in pain. But if you can love people of all kinds and of all classes, you will find that you will not only make a tremendous difference in the lives of people around you, you will find that you've been blessed by some of the most enriching and endearing relationships anyone could ever have.

Love cuts through it all. And it can be seen in a thousand different ways as people care for one another. But love does have a price. It's not always easy. And love can sometimes be emotionally confusing to one who is watching another suffer.

In the movie *Shadowlands*, Anthony Hopkins, who played the character of C.S. Lewis, befriends and falls in love with a woman named Joy Gresham, played by Debra Winger. Right after they are married, she finds out she has cancer and is going to die. After initial treatments, she gets well enough to come home—a real miracle. During this time, they enjoy some of the best days of their lives.

In this interlude of Joy's rebound from her cancer, they take a trip to Lewis' picturesque homeland where he grew up. During their outing, Lewis is relishing the time, and at one point he tells Joy how happy he is in the moment, not worrying about the past or what lies ahead.

"It's not going to last, Jack," Joy says.

"You shouldn't think of that now," Lewis corrects. "Let's not spoil the time we have together."

"It doesn't spoil it. It makes it real," Joy responds. "I'm going to die. And I want to be with you then, too. The only way to do that is if I'm able to talk to you about it now."

"I'll manage somehow. Don't worry about me," Lewis counters.

"I think it can be better than that, than just managing," Joy says. "What I'm trying to say is the pain then is a part of the happiness now. That's the deal."

In the movie, the two embrace and lock lips, and then, presumably, engage in conversation on a deeper level.

Like C.S. Lewis, many who care for a dying person are tempted to hold back on sharing their emotions with their loved one, because they realize that the greater the love, the greater the pain when that person is gone. But the wiser path of living goes the way of love anyway. Loving someone now is worth any pain of then, because love has a transforming quality that transcends time and becomes a part of both sides of the living and dying experience—enriching the quality of our lives and helping us truly live.

One such person who braved loving someone through a difficult experience was Cindy, a friend of Joni Eareckson Tada. Joni was paralyzed in a diving accident as a teenager. Today, she is a popular motivational speaker, singer, artist (painting with her teeth), and well-known advocate for the disabled. Her ministry, "Joni and Friends," touches thousands as she speaks and inspires people with her effervescent spirit.

However, she wasn't always so buoyantly optimistic. The first three years after her accident, she struggled emotionally as she adjusted to the rigors of being a quadriplegic. Cindy, who had stuck by Joni through the worst, was visiting one day when Joni was depressed and feeling sorry for herself. Cindy was fumbling for some way to bring encouragement to her. Philip Yancey writes that Cindy clumsily blurted out, "Joni, you aren't the only one. Jesus knows how you feel—why, he was paralyzed too."

Joni glared at her. "What? What are you talking about?"

Cindy continued, "It's true. Remember, he was nailed on a cross. His back was raw from beatings, and he must have yearned for a way to move to change positions or shift his weight. But he couldn't. He was paralyzed by the nails."

The thought so captured Joni as she pondered the possibilities that Jesus may have felt the same piercing sensations that now racked her body. And it put her on a quest that has helped her become who she is today.[5] This focus on the suffering of Jesus has been a therapeutic focal point for so many who have struggled with their own pain.

By now, millions of people worldwide have witnessed on the big screen the intense portrayal of the last 12 hours of Jesus' life in the mega-hit movie, *The Passion of the Christ*. Director Mel Gibson says that the movie was inspired by his own struggle with alcohol and thoughts of suicide. The turning point for him was when he began to meditate on Isaiah 53:5, "by his wounds we are healed." As he began to study and learn about the tremendous suffering and pain and sacrifice of Jesus for the sins of humanity, Gibson said it had a profound impact on him.

Why would focusing on such a brutally graphic scene be healing to anyone? I believe that for the hurting, it is comforting to know that through Jesus, God really does understand our suffering. He really does care for us. His love for us really is of the highest and most profound kind. To take the beatings and the pounding of the nails through His hands and feet for the love of the human race is mind boggling and deeply humbling to those who understand the magnitude and the personal application of that act. The last night that Jesus was with His disciples before the crucifixion, Jesus said...

> *"Greater love has no one than this, that he lay down his life for his friends." John 15:13*

Jesus then went to the cross and proved that He loved us with this highest kind of love. Paul, in his writing, calls this the "foolishness of the cross." He says...

> *For the message of the cross is foolishness to those who are perishing, but to us who are being saved it is the power of God. 1 Corinthians 1:18*

For many of us who struggle, if we ever get in touch with the mystery of Jesus' love that he demonstrated on the cross, we find the profound inner healing power that Mel Gibson and Joni found when they were captured by the reality of what Jesus did. Once I discover that Jesus' love is not just for the whole world, but a personal love for me, I feel a need and a desire to respond.

Going back to Phillip Yancey's observation that the best way to help a hurting person is to love him or her deeply, I am convinced that this is always the common denominator for those of us who are helping a friend or loved one through a tough time. We may not say or do the perfect thing for our friend, but our love can cover a lot of ground when it is sincere and sacrificial. Peter put it this way...

> *Above all, love each other deeply, because love covers over a multitude of sins. 1 Peter 4:8*

The love word here is another classic example of "agape" or sacrificial love. This is not necessarily a feel-good kind of love. But it is a love that can cut through all the junk and get to the heart. Peter, of all people, understood how powerful Jesus' love was. He denied Jesus three times and abandoned his leader during the crucial hours of the crucifixion. But Jesus reinstated him after the resurrection with three opportunities to express his love. Jesus' love got through loud and clear to Peter, and after that, even with his human foibles, the old fisherman was never the same.

That seems to hold true for others of the early leaders of the Jesus movement. John, who in his younger days was one of the "sons of thunder" with a quick temper, became a man on a mission to love deeply—reiterating that idea in his later writings. Paul experienced the same dynamic—being very judgmental in his younger years and writing of the importance of love in his later years. Clearly, as Peter, John, and Paul aged, love became a greater and greater theme for each one.

Today, I think we can see the full range of love in action as we strive to love like our spiritual forefathers did in response to Jesus' way of living. When we look at how love plays out, there are many subtleties. We can see the soft and nurturing side of love that brings chicken soup to our souls and makes us feel warm and cared for. We can see the hard and correcting side of love that cuts through our junk to wake us up and get us going in the right direction. We can see the sacrificial love that takes a hit for another. We can see the gracious love that allows someone to just "be" when they are not able to respond the way we want. Love truly does cover a multitude of sins—perhaps even our own sins when we try too hard in our own strength, power, or wisdom to fix someone else or make *them* feel better so that *we* can feel better.

Sometimes it's hard to figure out how to put loving feelings into action. Bill Burrows, my friend and partner in many interactions with hurting people, has a definition for love that I think helps us get to the heart of what to do when we don't know how to love someone. Bill says…

**"Love is being responsive to another person's reality."**

When Bill elaborates, he talks about how in any given moment we can be responsive or resistant to a person and to their reality. If we are responsive, we are accepting and at peace with the person. If we are resistant, we are at war and will hold off the person at arm's length. To highlight the body posture of this, when we are at peace, our arms and our hands are open to another. (Imagine opening your arms wide like you are about to hug someone). When we are at war, we have our hands up to shield us from the other person, or we have our fists ready to fight. In essence, our attitude can be one of peace and responsiveness, or it can be of war and resistance. In his letter to the Philippians, the Apostle Paul said that our attitude should be just like Jesus, and the imagery he set was of outstretched arms on a cross.

> *Your attitude should be the same as that of Christ Jesus: Who, being in very nature God, did not consider equality with God something to be grasped, but made himself nothing, taking the very nature of a servant, being made in human likeness. And being found in appearance as a man, he humbled himself and became obedient to death—even death on a cross!*
>
> *Philippians 2:5-8*

When Jesus stretched out His arms, He did it because He loved us. Similarly, when our attitude stretches our arms out, and we respond to our hurting friends, we are learning to love first with our attitude and then with our actions.

Bill talks about how any behavior can be done with a responsive or a resistant heart. Because we are human, we will never get it perfect. Often we can waffle between responsiveness and resistance even in the same interaction. The goal is to be as responsive as we can be at any given moment to both God and the other person. As we are able to do that, we will find that we are becoming better and better lovers. And to those who hurt, we are more likely to give them help that makes a difference.

Before we go too much further with this love talk, we need to remember the source of this love. As we keep coming back to this thought of how Jesus' love flows from the cross, I think it's important to take as many hurting people there as we can. If you are hurting, don't delay another minute. Run to the cross. Experience ultimate wholeness. At the cross, Jesus meets you with arms wide open.

While this message is one for the entire world, it has special meaning to a handful of survivors in a small Peruvian town in the majestic Andes Mountains. Let me take you there.

# Chapter Twenty-eight: Run to the Cross...

*"May I never boast except in the cross of our Lord Jesus Christ..."*
— Paul, Galatians 6:14

As I have mentioned earlier in the book, my parents were missionaries in Peru when I was a child. From time to time, our family would travel from our home in Lima to various places around the country where my dad worked or visited. Dad worked with university students on several campuses in Lima. A couple of times a year, he led the students to do mission projects in outlying regions. On one occasion, we drove deep into the Andes Mountains, winding through those mountains over the dusty dirt roads. In many places along that particular route, the road had no guardrails, and a slip off the road would mean a fall of hundreds of feet down the side of a mountain.

Dad's team of students was working in the region of Huaraz. I loved hiking up foot-trails to visit small churches in that area. And each time we reached a little church, we'd hear of another one "mas aya," further on.

One day, while traveling to another part of that region, we drove to a nearby town that was famous for a disaster that had struck there two or three years earlier. The town was called "Yungay" (pronounced yoon-guy).

Yungay was a picturesque little town at the base of a breathtaking mountain called Mount Huascaran. At over 22,000 feet, this mountain is snow capped and is one of the highest mountains in the world. For hundreds of years, the people of this region lived in great respect of that mountain. Many even worshipped it.

On May 31, 1970, at 3:23 p.m., a huge earthquake rocked the nation of Peru. Houses began to fall. Many people died in their homes. In Yungay, the disaster took on an added dimension. At the moment that the earthquake shook, it was like an explosion went off at the top of Mount Huascaran. And an estimated one million cubic yards of snow and ice burst into the air and began to flow down the mountainside toward Yungay, 11 miles away. As the snow and ice came down the mountain, it passed through lakes, and mixing with water, it created a mixture of mud, snow, and ice. The ice ground into the earth so much that it melted on the way down. Huge boulders were picked up and thrown into the air. Scientists estimate that at points along the way, that mudslide was coming down the mountain at a rate of 200 miles an hour. They calculate that it took about 4 minutes for it to arrive at Yungay. In minutes, the entire city was covered, and 16,000 people died. About 4,000 more died in another nearby town.

I will never forget that day when we drove into Yungay. It looked like a place from another world. We got out of the car and began to walk over the hardened mud that covered that town. Palm trees that once towered over the central city square were sticking out about 7 or 8 feet above the mud. As we walked over the town, we saw a few others that seemed to be doing the same thing we were. My dad struck up a conversation with one man nearby and asked him if he knew what had happened.

This man said that he was there on that fateful day. He was a member of a little church on the edge of town. He pointed over to a cemetery area on a hill. Originally, it was a cemetery built by the Inca Indians. But it was now a Christian cemetery. At the peak of it, there was a statue of Jesus with his arms outstretched. I could see that the path up to the top had crosses dotted to the side of the path. He explained that their little church wasn't far from the base of that cemetery. At the time, the hill was about 100 feet higher than the rest of the town.

When the earthquake hit, and they saw the mudslide coming, they looked to the cemetery and began to yell, "Run to the cross! Run to the cross!" And everybody knew what that meant. It meant that they needed to run to the cemetery—to the higher ground. That day, there were 92 people who ran to the cross and were saved. Everyone else died.

When I think of that story, I think of how Yungay is a picture of what the human predicament is all about. Whether we realize it or not, we all live at the base of a mountain of death that we can't predict. And just like the people of Yungay, we have a choice. We can run to the cross and be saved. Or we can do life on our own and perish. That certainly has implications for us when it comes to salvation, and I believe it has implications for us when we consider the suffering that we must endure in this life.

And when we talk of "running to the cross," we're not just talking about running to a couple of pieces of wood slapped together. We're talking about running to a Person. We're talking about running to the One who died on that cross and Who rose again—demonstrating that He had power over sin and death. And in that Person, we find life-giving power and guidance that we need to flourish in this life and ultimately in the one to come.

This resurrection power that comes out of the suffering of the cross has transformed millions of people since the days of Jesus. And it has the potential to impact generations to come. Through Jesus' resurrection power, the generations are connected, from generations past to generations yet unborn. To better understand this, I invite you to grab some 4-D glasses and turn the page.

# Chapter Twenty-nine: Back to the Future...

Marty McFly: *Hey, Doc! Where you goin' now? Back to the future?*
Doc: *Nope. Already been there.*

—From the movie *Back to the Future III*

"The future ain't what it used to be."[1]

—Yogi Berra

*The plans of the LORD stand firm forever, the purposes of his heart through all generations.* Psalm 33:11

*The LORD is good and his love endures forever; his faithfulness continues through all generations.* Psalm 100:5

*Even when I am old and gray, do not forsake me, O God, till I declare your power to the next generation, your might to all who are to come.* Psalm 71:18

*We will tell the next generation the praiseworthy deeds of the LORD, his power, and the wonders he has done.* Psalm 78:4

*All the ends of the earth will remember and turn to the LORD, and all the families of the nations will bow down before him, for dominion belongs to the LORD and he rules over the nations...Posterity will serve him; future generations will be told about the Lord. They will proclaim his righteousness to a people yet unborn—for he has done it.* Psalm 22:27-31

*******************************************************************

On a vacation several years ago in Florida, my family visited Universal Studios in Orlando, where we had a chance to see "The

Terminator." As we entered into the venue, we grabbed 3-D glasses and were led by a tour guide into experiencing the action of the movie. With our 3-D glasses on, the holographic images came into focus right before our eyes. It was so real looking, that at times I felt that I could reach out and touch Arnold Schwarzenegger or one of the villains who were right in front of my face. How they made something that came from a projector on the other side of the room create an image each one of us saw right in front of us is beyond me. But it does point out that sometimes it's good to get another perspective.

That's what I want to give you here near the end of the book. I want us to look at this world from a fourth dimension, from God's eternal vantage point. When God looks at His world, what does He see? Does He see a blue ball slightly tilted, spinning and orbiting around the sun? Yes. Does He see all the activity of our bustling cities with people going to and fro? Sure. Does He see inside the hearts and minds of every individual on this planet? Absolutely. God can see all these things—after all, He is God.

But God sees something more than all this. When God looks at this world, He can see all the generations of people—past, present, and future. In our limited vantage point, we only see our own generation. And more specifically, we tend to focus on our own little worlds with our limited tastes and preferences and our own small, finite worldviews.

But God wants us to be able to see even more than what we can see in our 3-D world. He wants us to occasionally step back and look at this world with one more dimension in mind, the dimension of being unshackled by time and eternity. I think God wants us to put on 4-D glasses and take a look at the generations with the added lens that helps us see people of the past, the present, and on out into the future.

We began this chapter with scriptures speaking to the fact that God's plans stretch across the generations—His love and mercy is freely given to every generation. But did you notice that some verses highlighted the desire of one generation to pass the torch of faith on to another?

Now, I'm no expert on this, but I understand that at any given time, six or seven generations of people are living at a time. (The experts vary some on this, so just go with me as I generalize a bit here). For example, in our day today, one of the oldest generations alive is the "GI" generation. This is the generation that fought World War II. Every day, thousands in this generation are dying. Next, is a generation that is sometimes called the "forgotten" generation, because it is squeezed between the GI's and the Baby Boomers, who were their offspring. Then we have generation "X" that is made up of those in their thirties. Then we have what some call generation "Y," and following that are the "Millenials," or some other designation of the youngsters of today.

Permit me for a minute to go into my church planter role and apply these truths and realities about the generations. When we look at the church, we can see a wide range of differences in the preferences of those in each generation. Have you noticed that? And have you noticed that in the church, walls of division and conflict can separate the generations—leading to gaps of perspective and ongoing turmoil?

Was this what God had in mind? Was a people divided by generational preferences God's preferred future for the people of this world? I think not. I believe that it has always been God's plan for one generation to bless another and for one generation to pass on their faith to another. Just look at those scriptures at the beginning of this chapter.

However, as a church starter, it pains me to see how generational differences have created divisions and misunderstandings in many churches—usually coming out of petty things like musical styles and such. I can't help but believe that this must tear at the heart of our Creator who loves each of these generations. Can the generations come together? Can we walk down a path of unity—even in the face of wide ranges of tastes and preferences in the way we experience life?

To answer that question, I want to take us back to Jerusalem on the Jewish holiday of Pentecost that we talked about earlier. Remember how Peter stood up to address the crowd when some thought that the followers of Jesus had too much to drink? Let's go back and listen in on Peter's message as he stood up on the highest step of the temple courts, and in a loud voice addressed the crowd.

*"Fellow Jews and all of you who are in Jerusalem, let me explain this to you; listen carefully to what I say. These men are not drunk, as*

*you suppose. It's only nine in the morning! No, this is what was spoken by the prophet Joel;*

*'In the last days, God says, I will pour out my Spirit on all people. Your sons and daughters will prophesy, your young men will see visions, your old men will dream dreams. Even on my servants, both men and women, I will pour out my Spirit in those days, and they will prophesy. I will show wonders in the heaven above and signs on the earth below, blood and fire and billows of smoke. The sun will be turned to darkness and the moon to blood before the coming of the great and glorious day of the Lord. And everyone who calls on the name of the Lord will be saved.'"*

*Acts 2:14-21 from Joel 2:28-32*

So much could be said about Peter's message, but I want to point out to you that Joel's prophesy that Peter quoted has a "generational" aspect to it. Joel had said that in the last days, when the Spirit of God moves, people of all ages will be getting in on the action— "your sons and daughters will prophesy, your young men will see visions, your old men will dream dreams..."

That wasn't always the norm. It wasn't the norm for younger sons and daughters to prophesy. It wasn't the norm for young men to have a chance to share a vision of a preferred future. And it certainly wasn't the norm for old men to rare back and dream—that was for the younger kids who hadn't had life knock the idealism out of their heads.

But in the early church, that prophesy of Joel was fulfilled. All these unlikely things happened. Men and women, young and old, they all experienced something together that is inspiring to look back on.

And as we look at this picture of the church, I can't help but wonder what our modern day churches could be like if the generations of our day were to work in harmony with God's plans and with one another. What if we dreamed of generational harmony?

What if each generation didn't just look after their own needs but looked up and down the age spectrum to bless other generations? What if older generations blessed the younger generations and the younger generations blessed the older ones?

What if some from the older generations looked at, say, the "Gen X" crowd, and in compassion said, "You know, not many churches are reaching out to these people. Can we bless a leader who is doing a good job at reaching them and offer resources to help increase the number of churches aimed at these people?"

What if those from the younger generation looked to those who are aging and said, "These people have done a lot to pass their faith on to us. How can we honor them?"

What if a church in the middle of a generational struggle over musical tastes stopped and began to ask, "How can we bless the group who is different from us?"

To even ask the question is hard for many of us to do on an individual level—much less at a church level. But I believe that it would honor God. Why? Because we serve a God who loves a thousand generations. And if He loves each generation, so must we. We should be putting on the 4-D glasses to develop God's vision and heart for people. And we should be seeking to pass our glasses down the line when it's our turn to get off this ride and let another generation rise up.

As we lovingly pass on our faith from one generation to another, many things need to be transferred. We need to pass on a healthy view of God, how to find Jesus, and how to be empowered by the Spirit. On a personal level, we need to pass on a healthy view of ourselves as fallen human beings, to show how to give and receive forgiveness, and how they can share their faith.

And, in all of this, I'd recommend one thing to fit into the mix somewhere. What is this one thing? It is our perspective on suffering. We must pass on to the next generation how to deal with tough times. Each generation needs to help the next generation get in touch with the suffering clause.

It may seem like a downer to tell people how to be ready to suffer. But to those of us who have lived it, we know that nothing else can keep us hanging on and joyfully living each and every day.

As I look at the generations represented in my family, I sense a connectedness to the flow of history that God is seeking to bring about through me as a result of my heritage. While this book began on a football field during my youth, a 4-D look at my life reveals God doing so much more—even before I was born.

I am the product of three generations of Baptist preachers. I see Dunk, my great-grandfather, passing the torch to Roy, my grandfather, who passed the torch to Don, my dad, who passed the torch to me.

So now I've got the torch in my hand, and it's my job to pass it to my kids, Josh, Zach, and Ryan, and to others. Maybe through this book I have had the privilege of impacting you, who now might impact others—perhaps even to a generation that is yet to be born, people you and I may never see.

As I look up and down the generational lines in my family, I see the normal range of suffering that every family experiences. There are illnesses, mishaps, misfortunes, death, and difficulties. No family is immune. But God gives us good news. He shows that He can transform our suffering into something that transcends our human experience and becomes something that actually produces a kind of joy we never thought could be possible.

My prayer is that this book would prompt a chain reaction of faith where tough times are not feared but embraced as a part of God's equation to bring us a "pure" joy that can be passed on to future generations.

As I pray specifically for you in these last pages, I have one more thing I want to share with you before I let you go.

# Chapter Thirty: Where Do We Go from Here?

*What if Your blessings come through raindrops?*
*What if Your healing comes through tears?*
*What if a thousand sleepless nights are what it takes to*
  *know You're near?*
*What if trials of this life are Your mercies in disguise?*[1]

—Laura Story
Chorus to song *Blessings*

By now we've covered a lot of ground in looking at a wide range of difficulties and trials we can face. Before we part ways, I want to make sure you have a vivid image of what it's going to take for you to be transformed by your tough times. To do this, I want to reinforce the "nail it" attitude I talked about in the beginning of the book and offer you something to focus on that will help you reflect on where we've been in this study and where we need to go from here. Incidentally, this is a part of what I sometimes do when I am coaching people through this material. I call it "The Ceremony of the Cross." Using a visual storytelling method, I guide you through the big decisions and the primary learning you've gleaned from this book. If you are going through this with a group, I urge you to use this imagery with each other so that you create a compelling, "nail it" vision for what the future can be for you and for each member of your team.

## 1. What is the most important thing in your life?

To begin this exercise, I want you to think about what is most important to you. What do you value more than anything in this world? Be honest about this. What do you want so much that at times it is stronger than your desire for God? If you can think of an item that represents this and that is located close by you, pull it out and hold it with both hands in your lap. For example, if your security is often wrapped up in how much money you have (or don't have), you might put your wallet or your purse out before you. If your family or a particular person is your greatest desire, you might take out a picture of them. Maybe your biggest aspiration is for a prized possession, or your health, or some goal, or a dream. If you need to pull out a piece of paper and write something or draw something, creativity *is* allowed as you determine what represents your greatest longing. Don't read any further until you have at least got an idea of what is most important to you.

## 2. Stand by Jesus' cross at Golgotha and listen to Him speak.

Now that you have your important thing in mind, I want to take you to a rocky hill outside the city walls of Jerusalem where all that we have talked about in this book comes into focus. Just a couple of chapters back, I implored you to run to the cross. Let's go now to a cross on Golgotha, the very place where Jesus was crucified, and listen to one of His most compelling pronouncements that He made prior to the crucifixion. As you hear Jesus' proclamation, use these words to remember what you need to do each day to be transformed by your tough times. Here is Jesus' unforgettable statement:

> *"If anyone would come after me, he must deny himself and take up his cross daily and follow me. For whoever wants to save his life will lose it, but whoever loses his life for me will save it."* Luke 9:23-24

## 3. Remember Jesus' perspective of not just looking *to* the cross but *through* the cross to joy.

When Jesus went to the cross, what was His attitude, and why did He do it? We've mentioned this thought a couple of times in the book. The author of Hebrews (Hebrews 12:2) said that it was "the joy set before him" that gave Jesus a frame of reference to endure the agony of the cross. The pain of the cross wasn't the motivating focal point; it was the joy that would come later. In essence, Jesus was not just looking *to* the cross, but *through* the cross. Like a field goal kicker looks through the uprights to where he wants to kick the ball, we look through the cross to the delightful reality on the other side. Jesus looked through the cross to a place where there was joy. Jesus could clearly see that if He endured the cross, He could experience the wonderful conclusion to God's redemption of mankind and bask in the happiness and the laughter of the resurrection. So as Jesus looks to His suffering, He is looking through it. To Jesus, the cross represented both His suffering and His joy-filled mission to save the world that would be completed on the back side of the cross.

When Jesus calls us to follow Him and asks us to deny ourselves and take up our cross, we find that the cross is the most appropriate symbol to capture both our suffering and how through it is *our* joyful, God-given mission in life. When we take up our cross, we embrace something that looks like death but in God's realm brings life and purpose. Remember that your suffering clause is tied to your calling to follow Jesus. But your suffering is not the end-all. Fulfilling God's assignment for you as you follow Jesus *is* the end. No matter how well you like the initial idea of your assignment, and no matter how hopeless the circumstances may appear, God promises that the conclusion to all the suffering will be joy.

### 4. See your little cross leaning against Jesus' big cross.

Now, let's get back to the exercise. You are approaching Golgotha with your most prized possession in your hand. When you get to the base of Jesus' big cross on the hill, you can't help but notice that leaning up on it is a smaller cross that has your name on it. As you look down at this, Jesus steps up next to you and says, "I want you to lay down your prized possession, and I want you to take up this cross with your name on it. There is pain and suffering involved in taking up this cross and accepting your mission that comes because of it. But I promise you that if you do it, I will be with you, and I will take care of you, and I will take you places you've never dreamed of. Drop what you have in your hand, take up your cross, and let's go."

**5. Lay down your prized possession at the foot of Jesus' cross and pick up your cross and embrace it.**

As you contemplate Jesus' invitation to walk with Him, you remember his previous words. "If anyone wants to follow Me, he must deny himself, take up his cross daily…"

As you ponder this proposition, all of a sudden the weight of the request falls on you. "Jesus wants me to give up what I hold most dear!" You muse in your mind, "I don't know if I can do that! And for what? To take up a cross?" Still processing your thoughts, you whisper under your breath, "Okay, let me get this straight, Jesus. I'm supposed to gladly trade my most important thing for a life of suffering and a big question mark? That's a lot to ask!"

But as you think about it, you glance over toward Jesus, and for a split second He locks His eyes on yours. With a piercing gaze and a nod, Jesus gives you a look of, "You can do this. This is the best thing you could ever hope to do."

So, with great apprehension you look down at your prized possession. Then you stare for a moment at the big cross. Then you glance one more time over at Jesus. He's still nodding that it's okay. With a quivering hand you carefully lay your cherished item at the foot of the cross. Then with a hand under each arm of the cross that has your name written on it, you slowly lift it up in the air to get a good look at it. With a shrug, you gently turn it sideways so it can rest on your right shoulder and you clasp onto the one arm of the cross that comes down over your shoulder. As you slowly spin around with the cross, Jesus moves toward you with arms wide open.

**6. Embrace Jesus.**

As you look into His face, you notice moist eyes and a tear trickling down His cheek. Then Jesus' mouth spreads wide as He breaks into an infectious grin. Without hesitating another second, you walk into Jesus' embrace—cross and all—and experience the bear hug of your Friend and your Savior. Somehow Jesus manages to hug you and get under your cross all at the same time. While Jesus holds you, you feel His warm tears drop on your head. After a lingering moment, you and Jesus turn to begin walking together.

**7. Begin your walk with Jesus.**

As you begin, you relish the interaction you have with Jesus while He talks more about what He wants you to do. You tell Him your struggles and your fears and your worries. Not once does He seem put off by your problems or concerns. For a few moments, you are so engrossed in the conversation that you hardly notice the fact that you are not the only one following Jesus.

**8. Join up with other cross-bearing followers in fellowship and encouragement.**

As you look around, for as far as you can see, you notice people with personalized crosses walking in the same direction you are. Many are clustered together in teams or with walking buddies. On closer inspection, these folks seem to be sharing their thoughts with one another and gaining encouragement and companionship out of the interactions. Some appear to be actually helping others carry their crosses.

"Hang in there," one calls to another.

"Can I help you carry that?" another says to a petite woman who is struggling.

Some cries seemed desperate. "I need prayer," one pleads.

"I don't know what to do," another confides.

"I'm hurt," still another confesses.

Other voices convey hopeful messages as you hear laughter and occasional squeals of delight.

Then someone comes up to you with a cross that looks like it's about the same size and with the same lettering as yours. If it weren't for the fact that the name on it was different, you could probably confuse the two crosses. "Need a walking partner?" the person asks.

"That would be great!" you respond, still a little in awe of the chain of events that seem to be rolling at you at a pace you can barely keep up with. As you reach out your hand and start to introduce yourself, you notice that your cross feels a bit lighter, and your heart is buoyed by a hopeful sense that God is connecting you to someone who might understand the burden of your cross. As you walk with your new partner, you both notice another person dealing with a similar cross. So you reach out with your right hand to introduce yourself to them. And so it goes...

*****************************************************************************

Let's press the pause button on the action. As tempting as it is to continue fleshing out this scene, I think we have seen enough of it to make a point and solidify our next steps. I know that I have taken some liberties to help us imagine the realities behind what happens when we decide to take up our cross and follow Jesus. I believe that this dramatic little clip I have created is consistent with the message Jesus conveyed. With this snapshot, we have a picture to use to diagnose where we are in our transformation process and then to know what we need to do next to match up with God's desires for us. Let me show you how this might work.

In this exercise, we first determined what we value most in this world. If this is truly what is most important to us, it will be the hardest thing we'll have to deny right now to follow Jesus. If we haven't gotten a clear idea of what this is, it might make our steps of self-denial a little confusing.

Maybe as we started the exercise and Jesus asked you to take your prized possession to the cross, you balked. From that point on, you might have been unwilling to go any further. In biblical language, this would be an idol. Until you are willing to give it up, this will be your biggest stumbling block to being transformed. No matter how spiritual we think we are, this denying of ourselves and of our idols will be an ongoing challenge for each of us. If you are stuck and can't seem to let go of what is holding you back, consider getting a trusted friend or a coach to help you through this. Remember that in the context of self-denial, when we say "no" to ourselves, we also say "yes" to what God deems is our most worthy pursuit. Don't let the marketing efforts of this world distract you from saying "yes" to God's ultimate place for you. There are no earthly possessions that can supersede the value of what God wants for you. Stay focused on what is really important.

Moving on in the visualization, when we stand by Jesus' cross and listen to His call for us to follow, I realize that some of you have never even heard and understood this call. If it seems really new or doesn't seem clear to you, you might need to take some time to understand what Jesus did when He died on the cross and paid the penalty of your sins. If you haven't figured this out, then make this your #1 priority, and seek someone you trust—maybe a spiritual mentor or a pastor to help answer your questions.

Next, we can see our cross leaning against Jesus' big cross. And with that we can ask, "Do we know what our little cross represents?" Put more personally, "Do I know what my suffering clause is, and do I have a clear sense of my God-given calling that is associated with my suffering?" Note that even though your suffering may be pretty straight forward, God's ministry for you that comes from it will likely develop over time. Your main focus for now is to trust that through the suffering God will usher in a joy-filled conclusion. If you haven't gotten clear on what your suffering clause might be for this season of your life, perhaps you need to take some time to ponder what this might be for you.

However, if you have a pretty good idea of what is important to you and can even name what your suffering clause is and have a hope that the cross represents a joy-filled future on the back side, you have a great foundation laid for being able to drop your valued prize and take up your cross.

When you do that and then have Jesus opening his arms to bear hug you, this is a good place to consider how close you feel toward Jesus. If you feel distant for some reason, or you feel like an unwanted child, this would be a good time to replace the lie you have been telling yourself with the truth. Often people struggle with self-esteem. If you struggle with this, I'd counsel you not to worry so much about your self-esteem. Focus on *God's* view of you. *He* esteems you and values you and loves you regardless of what you think or how you feel. There is nothing you can do to get God to love you more, and there is nothing you can do to get Him to love you less. His love for you just *is*! It is constant. Take some time to reinforce this truth in prayer and begin experiencing the closeness of Jesus.

As the movie continues to unfold, when we turn to walk with Jesus, perhaps you might feel nervous or unsure in taking your first steps with Jesus. That's completely understandable and normal. This is like other friendships; the more time you spend walking with someone, the better you get to know them. Enjoy the journey. Lean into the experience, and you'll be fine.

Perhaps as you went through the imagery, you were impressed by the camaraderie of fellow cross-bearers, and when you compared that with your current reality, you might admit that right now you feel isolated and alone in your journey. Walking with Jesus is not a solo sport. As we have alluded to in this book, we are a part of His family. We are part of His body. We need each other. Be quick to reach out a hand in friendship to another fellow Jesus follower. Make connection with others a high priority on your schedule. Remember that God called you to experience life with other believers who are also on the road to transformation. Along with reaching out to the already convinced, be alert to invite people who aren't a part of the family yet to come join you in your adventure with God.

When I explain this to my Kekchi Indian brothers and sisters, I hold out my hands wide and make my body into a cross. I ask, "Who is our leader? Yes, Jesus. He's the one who died on the cross and rose again. He invites us to follow Him and be a part of His family. So we become like adopted sons and daughters in the family of Jesus when we choose to follow Him."

Continuing in my explanation to my Kekchi friends I say, "Now, let's use this same cross to represent what we are to do as individuals and as a church." At this point, I reach up with both hands to emphasize the upward beam of the cross. "When we follow Jesus, one thing we do is connect with Him in prayer and worship." Then I point down with both hands and say, "The downward beam shows us that we are to be like a tree rooted in the ground. This is what is called discipleship. Discipleship is a word that describes how we are learning God's ways as we follow Jesus and are being obedient to what we learn. So this downward beam illustrates that we are rooted in God's word, the Bible. We learn God's ways together and we obey what we learn."

Then I hold my arms out again and say, "Our arms are open wide to love like Jesus loved. With one hand we reach out in fellowship to other followers of Jesus. With the other hand we reach out to invite someone else to join the family. Always use both hands to love people!

With one, love a brother or sister in Christ, and with the other love people who need to be adopted into the family like you needed to be adopted into the family."

As you can tell, I squeeze a lot of meaning out of the symbolism of the cross. I hope that this has been helpful to you and that this Ceremony of the Cross can serve as a visual aid to help you solidify the growth steps you've taken in your transformation process.

As you finish reading this book, I've got one more word of advice. Remember that being transformed by tough times is a daily exercise. Note that Jesus calls us to take up our cross *daily*. Unfortunately, this is not a one and done deal. Life as we know it will come with many opportunities to carry a cross and be in touch with our suffering clause on the way to fulfilling our mission in life. Some days the cross may seem like nothing. On other days, it may loom so big that we feel small and helpless under its shadow. But as we take up our cross and embrace Jesus in our tough times, whether our cross seems big or small, we find that God does something in our hearts that can't be denied. He transforms us from the inside out. He gives us the strength to carry our cross. He enables us to be more and do more than we might have ever imagined. He connects us to people who encourage and walk alongside us.

I realize that in raising up Jesus' vision of cross-bearing, the bar may seem way too high to get over. Many of us might be tempted to give up, because we know that our reality will never match up to Jesus' ideal. As a fellow struggler, I think I understand your hesitancy. I know that some days I will cooperate with God and gladly take up my cross, while on other days I will resist God and resent the pain and suffering in my life. Thankfully God offers grace and forgiveness and second chances. So don't give up. Every follower of Jesus struggles and falls. Keep on following. Keep on trusting. Keep on believing. Keep on connecting.

And that leads me to say again, if you haven't already downloaded some of our small group materials and used them as a springboard into discussions with others, I'd encourage you to go directly to our website at:

www.TransformedbyToughTimes.com

I believe this material could be used to foster conversations that draw people into becoming healing agents for one another. Are you open to the possibility that God might use your pain to heal someone else? Are you open to the possibility that someone out there is willing and able to help you find your healing? If so, then get a couple of others together for a group that can cross pollinate (no pun intended!) on these transformational ideas.

\*\*\*\*\*\*\*\*\*\*\*\*\*\*\*\*\*\*\*\*\*\*\*\*\*\*\*\*\*\*\*\*\*\*\*\*\*\*\*\*\*\*\*\*\*\*\*\*\*\*\*\*\*\*\*\*\*\*\*\*\*\*\*\*\*\*\*\*\*\*\*\*\*\*\*\*\*\*\*\*\*\*\*\*\*

To close the book, I want to share with you the complete lyrics to the song by Laura Story that I quoted at the beginning of this chapter. If you are not familiar with her, Laura has written many worship songs. One of her most popular is the song *Indescribable* that Chris Tomlin introduced to thousands of believers all over the world. Laura's song *Blessings* expresses the kind of heartache and questioning that I believe captures the hearts of many of us who go through tough times.

### BLESSINGS

We pray for blessings
We pray for peace
Comfort for family, protection while we sleep
We pray for healing, for prosperity
We pray for Your mighty hand to ease our suffering
All the while, You hear each spoken need
Yet love us way too much to give us lesser things

'Cause what if Your blessings come through raindrops?
What if Your healing comes through tears?
What if a thousand sleepless nights
Are what it takes to know You're near?
What if trials of this life are Your mercies in disguise?

We pray for wisdom
Your voice to hear
And we cry in anger when we cannot feel You near
We doubt Your goodness, we doubt Your love
As if every promise from Your Word is not enough
All the while, You hear each desperate plea
And long that we'd have faith to believe

'Cause what if Your blessings come through raindrops?
What if Your healing comes through tears?
What if a thousand sleepless nights
Are what it takes to know You're near?
And what if trials of this life are Your mercies in disguise?

When friends betray us
When darkness seems to win
We know that pain reminds this heart
That this is not, this is not our home
It's not our home

'Cause what if Your blessings come through raindrops?
What if Your healing comes through tears?
And what if a thousand sleepless nights
Are what it takes to know You're near?
What if my greatest disappointments
Or the aching of this life
Is the revealing of a greater thirst this world can't satisfy?
And what if trials of this life
The rain, the storms, the hardest nights
Are Your mercies in disguise? [2]

I pray that the perspectives you've gleaned from this book will be used to strengthen your faith, boost your hope, and give you the wherewithal to love people like you never have before. I pray that you live your days on this earth with conviction and purpose—especially as you travel some rough and rocky roads. May you experience God's presence, and may God's people rally around you as you go from this place. May you live well, love boldly, and finish strong in the race that God has marked out for you.

Your friend,
**Steve**

# IN GRATITUDE...

This book has been a long time coming for me. For many years, I said, "One day I'll write a book." Most of those times, I said it in jest after something had totally bombed—and those book ideas would fit in the category of *101 Ways to Blow Up Your Church* or *If At First You Don't Succeed, Maybe Failure Is Your Thing.*

Well, that all changed one day while attending the arts conference at Willow Creek Community Church. Rory Noland, the music leader there, spoke about how to encourage artists to do their craft. I was not there in the capacity of an artist but really as a chaperone for our music and drama teams attending the conference. (You know how those artsy people are!) In Rory's talk, he quoted Winston Churchill. Most are aware that Churchill was a great and inspiring leader of England during the difficult days of World War II. Many do not know that Churchill was also a painter. One day, someone asked him why he painted. "I don't paint to create a masterpiece," he said. "I paint because I love it."

After that, I realized God wanted me to write—not to create a masterpiece, but because I love helping people.

For this book, I also am indebted to Henry Blackaby and John Maxwell. In the summer of 2000, they both spoke at a conference I attended in Orlando, Florida. I honestly don't remember the specific words they said, but independently, both mentioned some things about the Apostle Paul that put me on a personal quest to understand what must have motivated Paul to last like he did in his ministry. That quest has become this book.

Similarly, I need to say thanks to Curtis Sergeant for sharing his heart about Church Planting Movements and how Christians in other parts of the world respond to suffering.

Along the way, many others have influenced me in big ways. My dad, Don Reed, has been a huge part of my life and ministry. My mom, Wanda, has loved me and rooted for me and prayed for me my whole life. I already mentioned my wife, Nola, in the dedication. My kids, Josh, Zach, and Ryan, have probably taught me more than I've taught them.

To my sisters, Lu Warren and Lana Reed, and to the extended Reed clan, Stephens clan, and more family than you can shake a Heinz 57 bottle at, I give you my thanks as well. To Nola's family on her Jones side, I feel lucky to have married into such a loving and encouraging family.

Thanks also go to people like Peck Lindsay, Sue Lindsay, Rick McGinniss, Charlie Baker, Carl Hunker, Adam Hamilton, Kenny Warren, Kelly Patterson, Rick Patterson, Chris Pinion, Cesar Gonzalez, Celso Midence, Greg Montague, Laurie Montague, Rod Casey, Bruce Dalman, Barbara Dalman, and others who believed in me and encouraged me when I was at some seriously low points in ministry.

Honorable mention goes to Jeanette Gardner Littleton and Mark Littleton, both professional writers, who have helped me learn some of the ropes in getting published. Meeting up with Jeanette's enthusiastic response to the idea of this book was a divine appointment for me. Also a huge debt of gratitude goes to Blake Elliott and Lee Warren, who painstakingly edited my entire manuscript for the first printing. Now, a sincere word of thanks must be expressed to Joyce Burrows for her remarkable abilities in proofreading and helping me improve this new version of the book.

I also need to thank Andy and Nancy Hagen, the gracious hosts of the Cedarly Pastors Retreat, who, along with other guests there, read the first pages of the manuscript and treated this rookie writer as if he were some world famous person.

I would be remiss if I didn't thank the people of Daybreak Community Church, who put up with me—warts and all, and allowed me to travel quite extensively on crazy adventures—all the while praying that we might become a part of a church planting movement in Central America.

Because this is the second printing of this book, I have had a lot of people read the first edition and help me spread the word. Without these faithful friends, I wouldn't be printing again. Since the first edition came out just as Hurricanes Katrina and Rita ravaged the Gulf Coast, for me, this book will be forever linked to memories of my friends who dealt with unimaginable adversity. Because of a generous gift, we were able to give over 800 copies of this book to pastors and church leaders impacted by the disaster. Some later wrote me to say that the book encouraged them. Today, those letters and emails are like golden treasures to me. Of my Gulf Coast friends, I want to say a special word of thanks to Joe McKeever, Jerry Bass, Steve Mooneyham, and to all the Baptist Associations and churches that invited me to come and speak to their groups after Katrina and Rita.

In more recent days, I want to thank Steve Harrison for sharing his wealth of knowledge and contacts with me. I want to thank the people of LifeQuest Church for believing in me and allowing me to minister with them and try out my small group materials on them. And I want to thank Bill and Joyce Burrows for allowing me to use them as guinea pigs for the concepts in this book and for helping me get better at coaching people through their tough times. I still have a lot to learn, and Bill and Joyce have taught me so much.

I also want to thank Paul Powell, Betty and Charles Alexander, Amanda McCanles-Crable, Rick and Linda Olson, Gary Snider, Ray Gurney, Karen Blankenship, and Keith Moody for adding their endorsements to the original book.

I want to thank my son, Josh Reed, for his excellent cover design and for his suggestions to improve the layout for this edition of the book. In addition thanks go to Jason Sears, who partnered with Josh to create a fantastic website for me and the book.

I know that I could try to mention others in my life who have helped me in some way or another. I have many friends in ministry who have walked with me through a lot of the ups and downs of my life. To those of you in that camp, you know who you are, and I love you all very much. Thanks everybody!

# ENDNOTES

**Chapter One: Think About What You're Thinking About...**

   1.  Tiger Woods, BrainyQuote.com, Xplore Inc, 2011, accessed March 29, 2011.

**Chapter Three: Singing in Jail...**

   1.  Lyrics to Elvis Presley's song, *Jailhouse Rock.*

**Chapter Six: Praying Dangerous Prayers...**

   1.  Oswald Chambers, *My Utmost for His Highest*, October 17th meditation.

**Chapter Nine: Jesus' Promises to His Followers...**

   1.  Philip Yancey, *The Jesus I Never Knew*, (Grand Rapids Michigan: Zondervan, 1995), page 107.

**Chapter Fourteen: Bold Love...**

   1.  Greek word definitions of "love" come from www.theologue.org, accessed November 9, 2009.

   2.  Analysis of "agape love" from www.answers.com, accessed November 9, 2009.

**Chapter Eighteen: Seeds of Greatness...**

   1.  Charles Colson, *The Body*, (Word Publishing Company, 1992) pages 218-223.

**Chapter Nineteen: The Suffering Clause Hall of Fame...**

   1.  Casey Stengel, www.thinkexist.com, accessed March 29, 2011.

2. Mike Evans, *The Unanswered Prayers of Jesus*, (Minneapolis, Minnesota: Bethany House Publishers, 2003), page 9.

3. Philip Yancey, *Where is God When It Hurts?* (Grand Rapids Michigan: Zondervan, 1990), page 19.

**Chapter Twenty: The Suffering Clause Hall of Pain ...**

1. Elizabeth Payson Prentiss, www.pastor.com, accessed March 29, 2011.

**Chapter Twenty-one: Where is God When it Hurts?**

1. *The Zondervan Pictorial Encyclopedia of the Bible*, (Grand Rapids Michigan: Zondervan, 1976), Volume Four, page 72.

**Twenty-two: Pain, the Gift Nobody Wants ...**

1. C.S. Lewis, *The Problem of Pain* (New York: The Macmillan Company, 1962), page 93.

2. Dr. Paul Brand and Philip Yancey, *Pain, The Gift Nobody Wants*, (New York: Harper Collins Publishers, 1993), page 4.

3. Ibid., page 11.

4. Ibid., page 12.

5. Ibid.

6. C.S. Lewis, page 93.

**Chapter Twenty-four: Unanswered Prayer ...**

1. From a line in Garth Brooks' song, *Unanswered Prayer*.

2. Henry Blackaby, *Experiencing God*, (Nashville: Lifeway Press, 1993), page 95.

3. Georges-Louis Leclerc Buffon, www.nonstopenglish.com.

4. Bill Hybels, *Too Busy Not To Pray*, (Downer's Grove, Illinois: Intervarsity Press, 1988), page 74-75.

**Chapter Twenty-five: The Guy Who Wrote the Book On Suffering...**

1. From John Ortberg's message delivered at Willow Creek Community Church on March 20, 2002.

2. Helen Roseveare, *Give Me This Mountain*, (Inter-Varsity Press).

3. Tanya Stoneman, from a personal interview of Helen Roseveare. Appeared on the website, www.suffering.net/thank.htm.

**Chapter Twenty-six: Hope with Your Name on It...**

1. Christopher Reeve, www.wisdomquotes.com, accessed April 1, 2011.

2. Tertullian, www.myfavoriteezines.com, accessed April 1, 2011.

3. Lee Strobel, *The Case for Christ*, (Grand Rapids, Michigan: Zondervan, 1998), pages 241-242. Used by permission of Zondervan Corporation.

**Chapter Twenty-seven: Helping Those Who Hurt...**

1. Mother Theresa, www.quotegarden.com, accessed November 9, 2009..

2. Philip Yancey, *Where is God When It Hurts?* page 168.

3.  Ibid.

4.  Earl Martin, *Passport to Servanthood*, (Nashville: Broadman Press, 1988), page 110.

5.  Philip Yancey, *Where is God When It Hurts?* page 134.


**Chapter Twenty-nine: Back to the Future…**

1.  Yogi Berra, www.quotesdaddy.com, accessed April 1, 2011.


**Chapter Thirty: Where Do We Go from Here?**

1.  Laura Story, chorus to the song *Blessings* on her album by that same title. Used by permission from www.musicservices.org.

2.  Used by permission from www.musicservices.org. For more information about the ministry of Laura Story see her website at www.LauraStoryMusic.com.

# ABOUT THE AUTHOR

Steve Reed is currently the Chief Encouragement Officer and Cross Cultural Catalyst for Daybreak International, a missionary entity he started out of one of the churches he founded. In the early 1980's, Steve played football under Jimmy Johnson at Oklahoma State University until a career-ending knee injury curtailed his athletic aspirations.

For over 25 years, Steve has been either a pastor, staff member, or lay leader involved in starting five different churches and helping others start churches that start churches. Steve networks with church planters all over the United States and has been strategizing with pastors and leaders in Central America on how to create innovative churches and ministries that are culturally relevant in their respective countries.

Currently, Steve is working closely with two different church planting teams. One is starting cowboy churches in Guatemala, Honduras, and El Salvador. The other team is starting churches for Kekchi Indians in the jungles of Guatemala. A few of these leaders were former communist guerrillas who have been transformed by a real and undeniable faith in Jesus.

In starting these churches and ministries, Steve has weathered some difficult and sometimes stormy situations. Yet, through it all, he has found compelling and joy-filled reasons to continue when many would have given up. Steve is married to Nola, and they have three young adult sons and a beloved daughter-in-law.

**To Schedule Speaking Engagements or to Contact Steve:**

www.TheSteveReed.com

**Steve Reed**
11628 Oakmont, Suite 102
Overland Park, KS 66210